PUBLISHING YOUR ART AS CARDS & POSTERS

The Complete Guide To Creating, Designing & Marketing

by
Harold Davis

THE CONSULTANT PRESS
New York, New York

PUBLISHED BY:
THE CONSULTANT PRESS
163 AMSTERDAM AVENUE
NEW YORK, NEW YORK 10023
(212) 838-8640

ISBN 0913069-22-1

Susan P. Levy, Editor

Printed and bound in the United States of America

Library of Congress Catalog Card Number: 90–081501

Table of Contents

ACKNOWLEDGEMENTS

I owe people too numerous to list gratitude for their support of my work as photographer, artist and publisher. That work has enabled me to create this book. Although the responsibility for the text is mine alone, I want to thank Eleanor Caponigro, Martin Davis, Irv Hansen, Marcia Keegan, David Lanham, Susan P. Levy, Lloyd Morgan, Robert S. Persky, Dan Poynter, Bonnie Reed, Gail Rice, and Conrad Stogel for their help in the creation of this book.

H.D.

1. Purpose of this Book

As an artist, I have "self-published" my work since 1980. My published work is photography, primarily landscapes, citiscapes, and evocative country images. The forms the publications have taken are as note cards (greeting cards with no captions inside) and fine art graphic posters (offset reproductions combining graphics and imagery). The term "self-publish" means to design, produce, market and distribute one's work oneself. In my case, my work is marketed under my company name, Wilderness Studio. Distribution of art posters is left to independent art distribution companies. Nonetheless, I still consider myself a self-publisher.

Over the years I have been consistently asked for advice in the area of publishing cards and posters. The typical questions include: How can I get my imagery published? Should I do it myself? If so, what is involved with starting a small publishing company? I have been asked to prepare talks on these topics, and I receive many phone calls asking for help or information. I have given workshops nationally along with Marcia Keegan, photographer and founder of Clear Light Publishers on *Self-Publishing for Artists*. By ideologic bias, as an artist, and as the President and co-founder of Wilderness Studio, I am a great believer in artist-originated, offset publications. I have several reasons for thinking this way. The artist may better understand the uses of his work. He knows how to design around it to create a unique product, and he is more committed to pushing it than a major publisher is. Often, major publishers will simply use imagery as part of the current formula for their line of products. And, in the absence of special factors, they will have no particular motivation to push the work of any individual artist.

However, many aspects of publication, such as distribution, involve great difficulties. Quite apart from any artistic merits, to successfully design, create and bring to market a visual product requires considerable technical business skills, much good luck, and plentiful financing. Furthermore, the artist may not be very good at judging the objective commercial viability of his own work when compared with a major publisher who deals with many artists, has a professional staff, and has had to stay competitive in the marketplace.

While my main field of expertise is the reproduction of photographic related imagery, these remarks apply to any kind of art. Firstly, the process of reproduction of any kind of two dimensional visual art is essentially similar. Also, marketing and distribution channels are either identical (i.e., the major art poster distributors generally carry work created in every original media), or, where there is specialty distribution, the business theory is the same. Finally, in the most general sense, the purpose of this book is to help the artist to think like a business person who is creating, marketing and controlling a product. In this sense, as one artist friend of mine put it, an artist is a factory who must also learn to deal with what happens to his product after it comes off the assembly line. By using this metaphor I do not intend to denigrate the beauty and magic of the creative process but rather to tell the truth about the kind of interaction with the world that is required to get the product to market. Technical business skills and an ability to sell and negotiate will go a long way towards helping an artist be financially successful whether he is self-publishing or marketing one of a kind sculpture. Finally, in my experience every successful artist or photographer has followed his own unique career path. Copying precisely what someone else has done will not work.

Many people who think they want to publish their own art work, or to start a card or poster publishing company, should be discouraged. Try to envision the consequences of the road you are about to take. Do you really want to turn your living room into a paper products warehouse? Card distribution is a full time business. Do you want to be a business person or an artist? Are you willing to make the compromises with your work that a business person must make? Can you put on business clothes, go out and sell, and continue to take joy in creating art? It can be much easier to stick to being the artist, either supporting it through other work, or letting an agent, manager, dealer or publisher handle the business end. The type of person who will be a successful self-publisher as well as artist will get pleasure from creating business as well as from the business of creating. This person must be skilled at the art of business in addition to the creation of art.

Finally, just as the true creative artist works in many media, the principles and illustrations in this book apply beyond the business of the creation of cards and posters. Those who are looking for input on "How to Start a Business" or "How to Produce and Market Any Product" will hopefully find some guidance.

In the following chapters I share what I've learned about publishing cards and posters from the points of view of both artist and publisher.

2. Clarity of Intentions

In most facets of life, the clarity of one's intentions has a direct relationship to the success in achieving the goals one desires. Possibly nowhere is this more the case than when contemplating a self-publication venture. What is the purpose of the publication venture? Is it to make money? To advertise a product, person or exhibit? To generate publicity for an artist or photographer? Is the main purpose aesthetic and artistic in nature? If the goal is to make money, the direction taken may be very different than when the purpose is of a public relations nature. In a profit-oriented publication venture, the ability to distribute is crucial. However, a distribution network, particularly in the greeting card industry, can become a hungry entity with its own priorities, constantly demanding to be fed with new material without regard for whether this is the most appropriate use of time, money and artistic urges.

If the main point is an advertising outreach, a good sense of who the target audience is and how you will get the piece to the target audience is vital and will change your design of the piece. It is not appropriate to put too much elaborate printing into a placard that will be pasted on urban walls and soon forgotten, covered with graffiti and pasted over. If the piece is to be mailed, cost considerations and the design of an appropriate mailing container become important. How do the costs and effectiveness involved in creating a piece for promotional purposes compare with those of other kinds of advertising such as directories? My own philosophy is to create pieces that are striking enough that they will survive in the marketplace, hopefully simultaneously producing income and advertising benefit. Although commercial distribution has produced some recognition for my name and imagery and for the name "Wilderness Studio", it is unlikely that I have received specific recognition from a market that might give me assignments or purchase my original prints. This has occurred where I have organized mailings or delivered copies of my posters in person. If you are interested in designing something specifically for promotional purposes please consider carefully the context of the piece. Art Directors do not have much extra wall space, and, unless it is very special, a poster will

3

probably end up being tossed. Also, if you are trying to get commercial work, try to send a piece which bears an intelligent relationship to the kind of work you are soliciting.

If your intention is primarily artistic, will you be able to realize your visual ideals when confronted with the realities of mass reproduction and the marketplace? Perhaps offset is not really appropriate, and you might be better off creating some form of limited edition print. Although the business issues involving production and distribution of prints are not totally dissimilar from those involving art posters, there are some differences having to do with higher unit cost, limiting editions and appealing to a smaller more discriminating market. These differences will not be fully discussed here.

Think about these things deeply before proceeding further. It would perhaps be a good idea to go somewhere outside your normal routine and "meditate" a little. Generate a list that indicates the objectives of your publication venture. Include intermediate steps, such as how you expect to achieve these goals and how you expect to achieve the intermediate steps.

The basic message is to plan. No doubt luck has a great deal to do with the success and failure of human affairs; over this we have no control. We can, however, to the best of our abilities, plan what we want to produce, what money it will take, where the money will come from, and how we will produce, store, ship, market and sell the product. There is no excuse for not having a well thought out plan, preferably in writing.

In connection with creating your plan, be sure to give some attention to timing. There are three important kinds of timing issues. First, what are the buying cycles of the industry? The distributors will place an order for art posters only when they are producing a new wholesale catalogue or supplement; depending on the company, this can vary from every two months to once a year. Holiday related cards are tremendously important to the greeting card industry, with a several month lead time. For instance, early January is the only "window of opportunity" for shipping Valentine's Day cards. Neglecting this factor can doom an otherwise excellent product to failure.

Second, what kind of overall product design cum social awareness trend is occurring? Factors that industry experts will speculate on that relate to this include: color, media, content and text. What makes pet rocks hot one year and plastic flowers that are sensitive to noise an "in" item the next? The fact of the matter is that both the card and the poster industries are very "fashion" conscious. In their own way they are as concerned with consumer and trade trends as the fashion industry itself. The moral here is that this has to be considered extremely carefully and in light of the recent and long term history of cards and posters, or whatever it is you are producing.

Finally, how does the product you are thinking of creating connect with your own business and artistic history? If it is successful, will you have the imagery in your library and money in the bank to follow it up with a sequel product? Is the imagery the kind of thing your buyers expect from you and are therefore prepared to buy from you?

I cannot emphasize strongly enough that the "art" of self-publishing an artistic product requires clear and focused thinking.

3. Different Hats

If you do decide to go into business as a small publisher of your art work as posters or cards, one trick I've found helpful is to think of yourself as wearing different hats when performing the different roles involved. These might be artist, designer, production manager, bill collector, accounts payable clerk, chief executive officer, salesperson, market researcher, to name a few. In a larger company different people normally play these different roles, and, as you can see, the characteristics needed to perform these different functions well are really quite different. As a case in point, consider how the sensitivity required to be an artist differs from the coldness required to successfully collect accounts that are past due. Here is where the different hats idea comes in. I remind myself that everyone in society is playing a role. I invent characters that I can "play" to perform the functions my company needs to have done. I have gone so far as to assign names to the different persona, suitably literary for the Director of Art Marketing and aggressive for the credit manager. (My Director of Art Marketing is "Julian Sorel" after Stendhal's hero; my credit manager is "Bruce Savage", "Savage" to convey the ferocity necessary for collection, "Bruce" after the various prominent Bruces in the fine art poster industry.)

Obviously, the owner of a small business, including an artist's self-publication business, is ultimately responsible for the way the business is run and for everything that happens in the course of doing business. I do not mean to imply that this can be evaded through the use of pseudonyms. However, there are a number of practical reasons for not appearing to be a one person operation (or, in any case, appearing to have a larger staff than you really do). Having someone who is not the artist sign the collection letters is very important. Also, having multiple "employees" is a great help in obtaining credit both of a business and a personal nature. A rule of thumb is to be very careful about granting credit to sole proprietorships; you can be certain your suppliers will consider this. It is also helpful to have someone who is not you around the office who can respond to queries regarding your income.

In all my years of operating this way, no one has challenged the same voice on the telephone with different names and job titles. I am afraid, however, that I will be in deep trouble if anyone ever insists on having me, Julian and Bruce to lunch simultaneously.

In the same vein, I understand that one of the richest businessmen in New York has answered the telephone as his own secretary under an assumed name for decades. It's certainly one way to know everything that's going on.

4. A Brief Business History of Wilderness Studio

In college, I studied painting and literature and then graduated with a degree in Computer Science and Mathematics. I have no formal education in photography. After college, I moved to California where I hiked the John Muir Trail and worked as a street cartoonist, a children's photographer and at various other odd jobs. I returned to the East coast and subsequently graduated from law school where I was a law review editor and wrote an article cited by the United States Supreme Court. I also worked in the general crimes unit of the United States Attorney's Office. But by this time it had become clear to me that photography was my calling. In retrospect, I consider my eclectic educational background a plus when it came time to create a card and poster publishing business. Many of the business people I deal with are pleasantly surprised to meet an artist who is also knowledgeable around business systems, contracts and law. If there is one conclusion I would draw from my experience it is that the artist who publishes his own work must learn to be a business person.

Wilderness Studio was founded in 1978 by Cori Falk, my ex-wife, and me when we moved into a loft in the Union Square area of Manhattan. The initial primary intention was to use Wilderness Studio as a vehicle for my work as an art photographer. During this period I taught myself to color print and started to have some success in the art world. The first real publications occurred in 1980 with a poster published by Modernart Editions and a postcard produced by *American Photographer* magazine (further discussion of this in Section 11, "Market Positioning") followed by a flat of postcards. A flat is the assembled composite of negatives or positives, ready for platemaking. Generally, cards will be printed a dozen or so at a time stripped together to make a flat.

I decided around this time that I was really interested in publishing my work in these media—cards and posters—for aesthetic, philosophic and practical reasons.

I had become interested in the offset process as an artistic medium and populist art form. By populist art form I meant that it was possible to produce beautiful objects and sell them at an affordable price. Also, how better to preserve the beauty of the earth and its wild places than by showing this beauty? I thought there was money to be made in publication, and that I could craft a career without becoming dependent on fickle art dealers or advertising agencies. Finally, it occurred to me that if I could distribute my product, it would be an advertisement for me and my work, even if I only broke even.

In 1981 I incorporated Wilderness Studio and registered the name as a federal trademark. I had several of my pieces published as posters by outside companies, and I started planning some ambitious pieces to be published as posters by Wilderness Studio. In the card arena, I published a flat of ten over-sized postcards and began forming a sales organization. I soon realized, however, that the capital and organization required to make a dent in the card business were formidable, and for a while I was stymied. Then I was approached by a large printing company who proposed a joint venture. They would produce a large quantity of cards and do the fulfillment and bookkeeping; I would provide the designs and imagery for a percentage of the gross. This arrangement worked fairly well for a number of years—there were some problems since our priorities involving such things as quality were not the same— and certainly built up the Wilderness Studio card inventory more quickly than I could have. Then the printing company sold out to a California conglomerate, who really didn't have much interest in Wilderness Studio, and through assertive exercise of my rights, I regained control of the inventory, which was delivered to me in several semi-trucks.

Meanwhile, Wilderness Studio had published a number of posters which were quite successful. Our "Dance of Spring" was an outstanding industry success, carried by almost all the distributors. This delicate image, in pastel pinks and whites, shows a creek in the Shenandoah Valley surrounded by the buds of early spring. It is almost, but not quite, a snapshot image, easy to like and certain to create that important feeling of wanting to be there. Probably the text running along the bottom of the poster, which states "The Dance of Spring is the Dance of Life" in a light grey italic typeface, has a great deal to do with the phenomenal success of this otherwise almost banal image.

In 1983, I went to Alaska for the third time and hiked alone across the Brooks Range. I got dropped off by bush plane, photographed rainbows, met talking bears, and when I reached a native village, they said to me, "Where did you come from?"

I went through a period of storing the inventory in my living room and manually processing orders, maintaining accounts and shipping orders. This became a full time occupation for me and several other people and just could not go on if I was to have time and energy to be an artist and create new products. Meanwhile I was producing significant quantities of new cards with higher production values than in the past.

My organizational problems were solved in two ways. Using my background with computers I was able to create invoicing, receivables, payables and tax record keeping systems that automated most of these areas (See Section 9, "Automating the Office"). I also decided to sub-contract out my warehousing and fulfillment needs to a professional organization which handled these areas for a number of companies. While there was some cost involved in this, and compromise, they surely did a better job of it than I ever could.

In 1986, the New York Graphic Society, the publishers of the Ansel Adams posters, agreed to publish on a royalty basis a series of posters built around my imagery titled "Country Images". At about the same time the Museum of Modern Art decided to purchase the unusually shaped (23"x76") vertical triptych "The Hanging Gardens of Zion" for sale in the museum store.

In addition to my publishing work, I have continued to sell original prints through art dealers, to accept photographic assignments and to consult on business issues.

Where is Wilderness Studio now? I am personally recommitted to my primary goal of growth as an artist. During the past year I have worked on a major project involving photographing people, developed my large format still life photography, and created imagery that combines my photography and painting. I continue to support the extensive sales of our successful posters and to responsibly and slowly add new imagery to the card and poster lines (as well as licensing my imagery to outside publishers). I am happy to essentially be a one person business again, and have made a decision to "privatize" the business, meaning to focus on artistic development and the creation of a superb and beautiful product, rather than to try to be all things to all people. I have no interest in turning Wilderness Studio into Hallmark.

5. Creating a "New Age" Business

Businesses are, to a considerable degree, a reflection of the personality of their owners. It is important to stand for something. We are not selling widgets; we are not a conglomerate; we are not Hallmark. We are making, marketing and selling reproductions of our art which reflect our creativity and our higher selves; therefore, let us stand for something. I need not love what you stand for but at least do it with individuality.

In my case, the values I have wanted to express via Wilderness Studio probably *can* be described in shorthand as "New Age": positive, spiritually open, delighting in beauty and in the beauty of nature. Quoting Napoleon Hill, "I believe in the power of desire backed by faith." Partly these values are expressed in my photography, in my published product, and in my willingness to share my experience so that it will benefit others. Where my business conduct has left room for improvement, I will try to do better next time. I believe that my customers understand my approach to these things, and it is partly what causes them to continue to desire to work with me and to buy the Wilderness Studio product.

Beyond the expression of these values in the product itself, tangible expression of them can be found in the name of the company (Wilderness Studio), the design of the typographic elements of the product, the packaging, and the oral and written communications with the customers. As described in Section 9 ("Automating the Office"), every sales commission and customer statement that goes out is headed by an inspirational saying which changes every month. I pick the sayings from my readings. My 800 number, 1-800-SKY-BLUE, is another example of value-based image construction. Be creative! Use your imagination!

This kind of effort plays a crucial role in image creation for a company. *Ben & Jerry* ice cream and *Celestial Seasonings* teas are two brands of products that have used

13

this to help create massive sales. Of course, both concerns had to have a good and viable product in the first place.

Right now, circa early 1990, a massive corporate leap aboard the environmental bandwagon is very noticeable. And what the public relations experts have determined is good for corporate America is particularly good for paper goods products where the essence of what is being created is image: the placement of posters on walls is a statement of personal or institutional values, and the delivery of a card conveys image information about the sender as well as a "personal" message to the recipient.

I believe that this—what I have termed value-based image construction—probably will not work if it is not truly felt; hollowness in this area can easily be perceived. Finally, a portion of your time or profits should be donated to causes in which you believe.

6. Deciding to Self-Publish

In the business world, it has become a cliche to state that distribution is the key to successfully marketing a product. Posters and cards are a product; they are so called "paper goods". It is a safe bet that as a fledgling "paper goods" publisher you do not have an existing distribution network. Therefore, you are much better off letting a company that already has such a network publish your work. That way you can get back to what you really do. If you are like me, I assume you have no secret yearning to be a big wheel distributor, or you would not have gone into art in the first place. You would have picked a business where there is real money to be made like screws, software or widgets.

One exception to this generalization is if you have something that is really hot, or steadily sells very well over the long haul. Then you will be very happy to publish it because if another company had, you might make comparatively little. (In cases involving smash trend hits that come and go, you may make nothing at all if you have the bad luck to be working with real operators.) What we are talking about here is the art world equivalent of hitting lotto. My poster "The Dance of Spring is the Dance of Life" has sold upwards of 25,000 to date (current retail $30.00) with no signs of sales slowing down. I am extremely happy that Wilderness Studio published it and that the outside publishers that I originally tried to interest in the piece passed. In rough terms, my net profit on the piece is $5.00 per unit sold. In comparison, my royalty would probably have been about .50 per unit had I worked with an outside publisher.

As Marcia Keegan notes, there are non-financial reasons for self-publishing. "When a large company publishes your work," she states, "you have given up almost all of your control. Self-publishing offers the rare opportunity to have a direct, positive and visionary impact on the world." Citing the example of her own company, Clear Light Publishers, Marcia notes that self-publishing can lead to publication of other people who you believe in who might not otherwise have had a chance to be published.

Nevertheless, initially it is probably a better idea to let someone else publish your art. If no existing company will publish your work, that is definitely a danger sign. Perhaps the work is not marketable. If someone else will publish your work, it is an opportunity, with no financial risk, to gain reputation and learn how the industry works. Finally, perhaps an arrangement can be struck where you are involved with creative aspects of product conceptualization and design.

One possible way to get started in self-publishing is to have an agreement with an outside publisher whereby after the term of the agreement expires the plates and film revert to you. (There are some options about the ways the details of this are worked out, but this gives you a chance to take over if the product is not selling enough to keep the initial publisher enthusiastic.) The publisher should be willing to agree to this because it costs him nothing. Perhaps some design changes (for example, in the case of a book to its cover) will cause the product to sell better at very low or no start up cost to you.

It is to be noted that if you are able to find a publisher, you will probably be offered a standard form contract. For a first publication, it is all too likely that this contract will offer very little financially. While it is possible that this will be essentially a take it or leave it proposition, be aware that an offer of a contract is simply that, e.g., an *offer*, which you may use as a starting point for negotiation. Do get it in writing, and do check out the credentials of the company you will be working with. Make certain it has an ongoing preferably computerized method of reporting sales and royalties and try to talk with other artists the company has worked with. Also, get a sense of what the going rate is for the "stock" usage of your image for the product and scope of rights involved. A good starting place for this is the current edition of the ASMP *Stock Photography Handbook*.

7. How to Find a Publisher

There are many ways to go about locating appropriate publishers. Some are suggested in this section. If your material is basically marketable, (and what this means is that there is a real way that real people will actually buy it at a price for which it can economically be produced) then, given a few assumptions, you will find a publisher. What we are assuming is that you are persistent (I am in essential agreement with Thomas Edison's formula that life is 98% perspiration and 2% inspiration), polite, do your homework and are generally professional. Professional organizations such as the American Society of Magazine Photographers (ASMP) or Graphic Artists Guild can help you learn professionalism through their guidelines and through contact with other members. If there are workshops relating to the appropriate markets in your area, this might prove to be very helpful.

You can find an agent to take your work to publishers. This might be a personal photographer's or artist's rep, or it might be a "stock" agency. Photographic stock agencies regularly sell imagery to greeting card companies. (Some agencies also handle illustrations.) It is the easiest thing of all to give your work to such an agency and let them do the rest while you go out and take more pictures.

A very good move is to spend a lot of time in your favorite card and poster stores. Note who publishes material that is related to yours. Study the poster catalogues which are readily available for inspection at most graphics galleries or framing shops. Most publishers are sure to put an address on their product. Then contact these publishers and find out whether and in what form they wish to see submissions.

Trade shows are an excellent opportunity to see who is publishing what. Use the trade show to make notes and to do very preliminary contact with potential publishers. Never harass the exhibitors at a trade show, as they are at the show to sell, not to buy, and too much hard sell on your part will be counterproductive. Probably the art director or photo editor is not even at the show. Find out his or her name and write inquiring about submission procedures. By all means obtain the exhibit directory as this is a valuable reference tool. Artexpo in New York in April is the most important fine art graphic poster trade show that I know of. The National Stationery Show (NSS) in New York in May is the leading greeting card and paper goods show in the world. Also important are the various Gift shows. There are some important trade shows on the West coast as well.

Trade publications can give you valuable information about the timing of the shows. Additionally, their editorial and advertising content will perhaps enable you to zero in on the right publisher. In the art poster field, you might look at *Decor* and *Art Business News*. In the paper goods area, check out *Greetings*.

There are also various kinds of directories which provide some information on potential buyers of paper goods projects, such as *Photographers Marketplace* and *Artists Marketplace*, although I am not persuaded that these listings are either accurate or complete. Check out your Business Yellow Pages under "Greeting Cards" and "Posters". Word of mouth and "networking" with other photographers and artists are potentially valuable ways to get information about publishers. Some of the major purchasers of art for use as cards and posters are listed in Appendix II and Appendix III at the end of this book.

In addition to practicing professionalism in the initial stage of contacting potential purchasers of your work, avoid future trouble and continue to operate as a professional when you submit work and if any work is actually used. Please be aware that when you "sell" imagery, what you are generally doing is licensing rights to use the imagery in certain specified limited ways. For example, you may grant someone "one time North American rights to reproduce as a poster in a press run no greater than 5000 for two years". Only very rarely, and for a substantial fee, should all rights and the copyright to an image be sold.

Submissions of imagery should be accompanied by a Delivery Memo, such as the one reproduced in the *ASMP Stock Photography Handbook*, that protects you by including loss and damage provisions and prohibits reproduction in the absence of your paid invoice. A reproduction of the Delivery Memo I use appears as Figure 1. Your invoice should clearly state what reproduction rights are licensed. A reproduction of the invoice format I use for licensing imagery appears as Figure 2. Keep copies of all paperwork.

DELIVERY MEMO

From: Harold Davis   Date: To:
            Wilderness Studio
            299 Pavonia Ave.
            Jersey City, NJ 07302
            201-659-4554; 800-SKY-BLUE

Enclosed Please Find:

Subject/Description	Format:	35	4x5	cont	oth	Value

Kindly check count and acknowledge by signing and returning one copy. Count shall be considered accurate and quality deemed satisfactory for reproduction if said copy is not immediately received by return mail with all exceptions duly noted.

Total Black & White:

Total Color:

Terms of Delivery:

1. After 14 days the following holding fees are charged until return: $5.00 per week per color transparency and $1.00 per week per print. 2. Submission is for examination only. Photographs may not be reproduced, copied, projected, or used in any way without (a) express written permission on our invoice stating the rights granted and the terms thereof, and (b) payment of said invoice. The reasonable and stipulated fee for any other usage shall be three (3) times our normal fee for such usage. 3. Submission is conditioned on return of all delivered items safely, undamaged and in the condition delivered. Recipient assumes insurer's liability, not bailee's, for such return prepaid and fully insured by bonded messenger, air freight or registered mail. Recipient assumes full liability for its employees, agents, assigns, messengers, and freelance researchers for any loss, damage or misuse of the photographs. 4. Reimbursement for loss or damage shall be determined by the photograph's value which recipient agrees shall be no less than a reasonable minimum of $1500.00 for each transparency and $100.00 for each print except as noted above. 5. Objection to these terms must be made in writing within five (5) days of the receipt of this Memo. Holding the materials referenced herein constitutes acceptance of these terms. Article 2 of the Uniform Commercial Code is hereby incorporate by reference into these terms. 6. Any dispute in connection with this Memo including its validity, interpretation, performance or breach shall be arbitrated in New York, N.Y. pursuant to rules of the American Arbitration Association and the laws of the State of New York. Judgment on the Arbitration award may be entered in the highest Federal or State Court having jurisdiction. Recipient shall pay all arbitration and Court costs, reasonable Attorney's fees, plus legal interest on any award or judgment. 7. Recipient agrees that the above terms are made pursuant to Article 2 of the U.C.C. and agrees to be bound by the same, including specifically the above Clause # 6 to arbitrate disputes.

* * * * * *   **ACKNOWLEDGED AND ACCEPTED:**_____

Figure 1

Harold Davis
Wilderness Studio
299 Pavonia Ave.
Jersey City, N.J. 07302

To:

INVOICE

Account #

Invoice #   **Terms: Net 30 Days; Past Due Invoices will**
be charged 1.5% interest per month or fraction thereof.

_____

TOTAL AMOUNT DUE: $

Except as otherwise specifically provided herein, all photographs remain the property of the Photographer, and all rights therein are reserved to Photographer. Any additional uses require the prior written agreement of Photographer on terms to be negotiated. Unless otherwise provided herein, any grant of rights is limited to one(1) year from the date hereof for the territory of the United States. The grant of the license stated above is conditioned upon (1) an appropriate credit line and (2) payment of this invoice in a timely fashion.

Figure 2

8. An Overview of Self-Publishing

Despite all the words of warning in Section 6, "Deciding to Self-Publish", there are some good reasons to start your own card or poster publishing business. Foremost among these is that you feel you have valid ideas or imagery and can't get a publisher. The desire to have control of your own artistic expression and to have an impact on the world are other positive motivations. Perhaps no existing publishing company will handle your work in the way, or with the quality production and design, that you feel they should. Please bear in mind, however, that the failure rate for new "paper goods" publishing businesses is even higher than that of new businesses in general, and also any start up business is a monster that takes all of your available time. If publish you must, you will need to consider the following topics:

- ☐ Business Organization
- ☐ Image Selection or Creation
- ☐ Market Positioning
- ☐ Financing
- ☐ Production
- ☐ Fulfillment
- ☐ Distribution
- ☐ Managing Cash Flow, Receivables and Payables
- ☐ Integrity and Ultimate Goals.

What do these terms mean? *Business organization* involves how you will handle orders, keep track of them, and who will do all this. Proper records must be kept for tax purposes. *Cash flow* is how much money you have in the bank, *accounts receivable*

21

is money owed to you, e.g. by card stores, and *accounts payable* is money you owe for goods or services, e.g. printing. If your publication business is to grow to any size at all, you will need to hire competent people to help with this, or computerize these functions, or both. *Payroll* is seeing that the competent people who help with this are paid regularly so that they continue helping. Finding and keeping good help is one of the most difficult things for a small business to do (also see Section 3, "Different Hats").

Image selection (and/or creation) involves finding or making the right images or designs to appear on your product. In a larger sense, this involves having the right *idea* for a product line. Again, without a real product that real people want to buy, you have nothing. That means that this is the most important part of all.

This is an area in which feedback from qualified people will be particularly helpful, as we are often not particularly able to be objective about our own imagery or work we are deeply involved with. You might consider joining or forming a support group to help with this, or participating in a workshop.

Luck, timing and larger social trends play a big role here. What's hot and what's not will make or break ventures. Environmental consciousness was big in the late eighties. What will the coming years bring? You can be certain that any good idea will be imitated. Also, almost any product line you can conceive of has a sales saturation point, or ceiling. Beware of printing more of your imagery than anyone will ever buy.

What makes a visual product successful? Distinguished designer Eleanor Caponigro suggests, "a magic formula that nobody knows."

Market positioning covers what your product is, who you will sell it to, and how you will sell it. For example, Wilderness Studio publishes blank photographic note cards and fine art graphic posters. Our market consists of visually sophisticated people, many of whom reside on the East or West coasts, who enjoy nature. Our posters largely end up in such places as corporations, hotels and hospitals and are chosen by interior decorators and professional art consultants. A full analysis of this, as you would have to make before introducing a new product, would be a great deal more extensive. Plan to do this and to produce a written marketing proposal. Lloyd Morgan of Morgan Press, who wears several hats as both a high quality commercial printer and a publisher of photographic books and specialty cards, suggests careful analysis of the competition. He notes that production values of your product must be comparable to the competition.

Simply put, *financing* is the method you will use to finance the production of your product and the overhead of running your business. If you have a substantial trust fund, this will not be a problem. Otherwise, considerable thought and work will be required. A business plan is a necessity. You will have to project sales and income. Try to be realistic about when you will actually collect the money you are owed from sales (see the section below on collections). In addition to financing the costs of your product, you will also have to make provision for covering your overhead until your collections allow a margin for this. The first allocation from cash collections probably will be to cover production costs. Sober planning suggests putting aside appropriate amounts to cover pro-rata reprinting and future production. In the meantime, where is money for the phone bill and rent coming from? Generally, it is very difficult (read: next to impossible) to finance start up or expansion from cash flow.

Production is the process of physically creating something, starting from the design and progressing through the printing and *post-production* (this means such finishing touches as binding, folding and packaging). For further discussion of this see Section 13, "Production".

Fulfillment means storing inventory and packing, shipping and sending orders to wholesalers, retailers or retail customers.

Distribution and marketing involves the creation of the sales process: how are stores or wholesalers convinced to carry the product? How is a chain of sales and shipping created so that the goods are in the right places at the right times? How is a product created for which there is a market?

American business is based on the keystone markup system. In theory, this means that each entity whose hands the product passes through doubles the price. For example, take a fine art poster that retails for $30.00. (Let us note here that retail prices cannot be arbitrarily set. For the small publisher they are pretty much compelled by prevailing prices for similar products already on the market.) This means that graphics stores and art galleries (the retailers) are selling them to the public for $30.00, plus, of course, framing. The retailer, in turn, is buying the poster for $15.00 from the distributor (also termed wholesaler). When the product is created by a small publisher, the wholesaler purchases it for $7.50.

The implication for the self-publisher is that he will need to generate a multi-tiered pricing structure. It is neither ethical nor good business to undersell your distributors or retailers. The same poster should be sold at retail to an individual for $30, at wholesale to a store or dealer for $15, and to a distributor for $7.50. The same general principle applies to the card industry, and indeed, any industry. Of course, minimum quantity requirements will apply to trade and distributor orders.

Incidentally, the $30 illustration is fairly typical for the art poster industry at the date of publication of this book. The keystone markup, or discount, system generally applies, with some downward negotiating based on payment agreements and quantities involved. Over time, these downward pressures are counteracted by the publisher, who will raise his prices every few years. Also, retailers can often get better prices on the pieces the distributors have created themselves due to the greater profit margin on these.

A sales commission, in the card industry normally between 10% and 20% of wholesale, will be paid by the distributor to an "outside", or independent, sales rep. Generally, in the card business the small publisher will be functioning as his own distributor and as such will be responsible for commissions.

If you do not know what *integrity* is, there is probably very little I can tell you about it here. My primary concern is with product integrity, not ethical integrity, and my belief is that the consumers of posters and cards do look for integrity ("quality"). I therefore feel that if you do not believe in your product (1) you should not be producing it, and (2) it probably will not sell. As Eleanor Caponigro notes, "The public responds to things that are well done. It's hard to distinguish yourself in a crowd of mediocre products. Given a choice, people will choose the better produced." As discussed elsewhere, production and design are inter-related. Intelligent production need not be expensive if it is well designed and appropriate.

Let us take time out here to mention two important points. Your product must carry a proper copyright notice. Generally, this should be in the name of the artist and consists of the (C) with the circle around it followed by the copyright name followed by the date. For example: (C) Harold Davis 1990.

Also, if you publish a product with a recognizable image of any person, you must have a valid release from that person. Some discussion of model releases and sample forms to use appear in the ASMP's *Professional Business Practices in Photography*. You probably should also get releases for recognizable real or personal property, for example a classic car.

Any questions about copyright notice or model releases should be resolved by consultation with qualified experts.

This overview will perhaps have begun to give you an idea of the many facets involved in publication. Hopefully, it will have helped dissuade those of you for whom starting a publication or self-publication (the difference being whether the venture is primarily a vehicle for your own art work or that of others) is of only passing interest. Remember to bear in mind the various possible functions of, for instance, a poster besides its marketability as a product. A poster may be intended to get a message across, announce a new product, or promote an artist. What is the intended function of your product?

9. Automating the Office

The topic of this section is computerization. Timely computerization of the small business is vital in order to: (1) conserve creative energy; (2) avoid high overhead through excessive salary payments; (3) generate quality business organization and paperwork; and (4) be prepared to handle success. Today, a fairly modest investment in software and hardware enables a small business to produce work that is on every level competitive with what the largest corporations can generate. In my opinion, this is a wonderful and glorious state of affairs. However, before attempting to automate your business systems, it is *absolutely essential* that you have a manual system in place which works and which you personally understand every step of the way. It is better to have a solidly working manual business than a computerized mess. The intention of the presentation of my sales system, which follows, is *not* to provide enough information here to create a similar system yourself. What it does provide is a starting place, a bare bones outline of the functions you will need to implement first manually and then electronically. This is an important component in the specification of a system. Your options (obviously there are trade offs each way, and your best choice depends on your individual situation, resources, abilities and requirements) are: (1) find an expert and pay him to develop and implement a system according to mutually agreed upon specifications; (2) research existing sales software packages and buy (actually, license) the one closest to your needs; or (3) learn enough about accounting, business systems, computers, software and a relational database language to create your own system.

The key concept is that an automated business system (and, actually, this is true of a manual one as well) is an issue of design in the same way that the creation of a successful poster, card or chair is an act of design. Computers do not just process numbers; within the limitations of memory and speed of your configuration, anything you can conceptualize with rigorous clarity can be processed. Simplicity, clarity of thought, bullet proofing (also known as fool proofing), and good documentation will win the day.

Also, let us note up front that the issues involved are those of software and not hardware. You need not have state of the art equipment. Basically, I would suggest as a hardware minimum a DOS machine with 640K of RAM, a 20mg hard disk, and a dot matrix printer. If you are interested in purchasing an industry specific complete software package, be very sure to take it for a thorough test drive before purchasing.

Wilderness Studio Sales System

© Harold Davis 1987

a. Exit from System

b. Enter Invoice

c. Generate Invoice

d. Post Invoice

e. Post Payment

f. Enter Credit/Debit Memo

g. Generate a/r schedules

h. Generate Statements or Past Due Notices

i. Generate Sales Commission Statements

j. Print cash receipts journal

k. Add new account

l. Update list of Sales Reps

m. Update stock items of inventory

n. List Accounts

o. Analysis of Accounts by Sales Rep

p. Change Slogan of the Month

Please enter a Code:

Figure 3. *Wilderness Studio Sales System Menu*

The basic business functions that I use my computer for are word processing (WordPerfect); mailing lists (dBase III, a database language); invoicing, accounts receivable, and commissions (custom created software in dBase III, see discussion below); and check writing, accounts payable and tax record keeping (custom created system; there are many good ones commercially available such as *NuViews* or *One-Write Plus*).

There will be no further discussion here of word processing, which handles correspondence, business forms unrelated to an inventory, invoices of a non-routine nature and collateral matters. Likewise, mailing list handling is straight forward enough, whether you use a database language to create a system for handling your lists or purchase a commercially available stand alone program. The point of having an automated check writing system is that this will enable you to keep track of bills as they come due, to keep your accounts reconciled, and to post into general ledgers and cash receipts and disbursements journals. These should be used to make life easy at tax time and to generate appropriate financials for obtaining financing and for business planning. My own current approach is to keep my business manageable in size so that I don't have to cope with a large overhead. I spend about five hours a week on my automated bookkeeping systems. While at some point (if your intention is to expand your business) you will want to delegate these functions, it is vitally important that you understand them all first. In any case, it is my belief that until a business is large enough to have a responsible financial control officer, the beneficial owner should personally sign all checks. Essentially the payables side of the business does not vary much from business to business; however, the receivables side, i.e., order taking, invoicing, etc., does. What follows is a discussion of the Wilderness Studio system, which is based around interlocking databases of accounts, inventory items, invoices, and sales reps. Please see Figure 3 which illustrates the Main Menu of my design for handling these issues. Hopefully, following the options on this menu will enable the reader to gain a broader understanding of the business system issues because this understanding is more important and more to the point than software considerations. If it can be conceptualized with clarity, it can be made to work in your computer.

A brief note on computer consultants. While at the beginning some expert help will probably be needed, be extremely careful about this. Not only are they expensive, but it is also sometimes in their interest to encourage overly grandiose automation schemes and dependency on their expertise. There are many consultants around, but not that many good ones. Try to make sure you learn what you need to know yourself, and if you do not understand something, remember that it is never foolish to ask questions.

What follows is a brief discussion of the Wilderness Studio Sales System Menu (see Figure 3). The reader who is not at the point of organizing a sales operation might wish to skip to the next section.

Option (a) is the exit from the system. Option (b) allows the user to create an electronic version of a new invoice. If a new account is involved, the user enters new account information such as billing address, shipping address and the code for the sales rep. If it is an invoice for a previously initialized account, the information is pulled out of the account database. A new invoice number is assigned. The user is then requested to enter some information such as the terms of the order, purchase order number, if any, and how to ship it. Finally, the user interactively flags the quantity and stock numbers of whatever is to be shipped. The program pulls up descriptions of the inventory items and unit prices from the inventory database, totals the prices, requests shipping costs and discount, if any, inquires if any special message goes with the invoice, totals the invoice and stores it in a file.

Option (c) generates a hard copy form of the invoice. I use a carbonless quadruplicate blank form (obtainable from Moore Business Products, see Appendix I, "Resources") which I run through an inexpensive dot matrix line printer used only for business forms set up on a switch box. Two copies go to the customer, one goes in my hard copy account file, and one goes in my annual file of all invoices, sorted by type. Option (c) and the blank forms are also used to generate a hard copy "Shipping Document" with the same content as the invoice except that only the shipping address is indicated and there are no prices marked. The shipping document is sometimes referred to as a "Bill of Lading" or a "Packing Slip". In my case, I simply mail three of the four copies to my fulfillment warehouse which sends a copy with the packed order to my account. The customer will compare the contents of the shipment with the shipping document, which states, "Please examine merchandise at once and report any damages or discrepancies," and the invoice, which is formatted to fit in a window envelope and arrives by U. S. Mail. Accurate, clear and consistent paperwork helps to insure timely payment by eliminating the possibility of misunderstandings, intentional or otherwise.

Option (d) posts invoices "to all relevant databases", which means to the file of all invoices, to the file for the individual account, to the accounts receivable journal for the type (poster, card or miscellaneous) of account, and, if applicable, to the file for the commissionable sales rep who services the account. Functions built into the dBase language will then allow me to quickly inspect any of these records should I need to know, for example, the status of an account. Option (e) posts payment to the same relevant databases. Option (f) is used to enter credit or debit memos, mostly in my case credit for damaged posters. As noted in the discussion on fulfillment, damages are inevitable in shipping posters and must be calculated into inventory cost. Option (g) is used to generate hard copy of the accounts receivable journals and aging of accounts receivable, either overall, by type, or by account.

Generation of statements, past due notices and dunning letters is handled by option (h). Each of the forms can be printed for a specific account, or for all accounts that have appropriate open or past due balances. (See Figure 4, page 58, for a sample letter.) All forms clearly list the amounts due and are configured to fit in window envelopes.

Sales commission statements are handled by option (i). While individual commission statements can be generated, I usually proceed automatically with statements for all the sales reps. Accounts are listed on the statement as "Shipped but not Paid", or "Paid". A commission is calculated on paid accounts, and the file for the account is marked that the commission has been paid. Again, the form fits right into a window envelope.

Option (j) prints a month by month cash receipts journal, pulled from the payments which have been posted. While I use my accounts payable system as my primary tax record keeping system (after all, it is clear that what is deposited is a cash receipt), having this kept track of here does serve as a confirmation. Options (k), (l) and (m) allow additions and changes to the accounts, inventory and commissionable sales rep data bases.

Current accounts are listed by option (n) along with their account number, address, type and sales rep code. Option (o) provides analysis of the account performance of the sales reps.

All my statements to accounts and sales commission statements contain an inspirational quotation that changes every month (See Section 5, "How to Create a New Age Business"). Option (p) allows me to change the quotation.

Hopefully, the above helps to provide a fairly thorough albeit not complete summary of systems needed to handle the receivable side of the small publishing business and how they might interact with a computer. Illustration of my specific systems, while not the only way to go about it, at least gives an indication of the functions that will need to be covered and provides a starting place. Systems may also have to be provided for accounts payable, tax record keeping, check book management, advanced inventory control, and payroll.

Finally, a computerized system and hard disk is Murphy's Law waiting to happen. Back up everything essential to your business both on hard copy and on disk.

Wilderness Studio, Inc.
299 Pavonia Ave.
Jersey City, NJ 07302
201-659-4554; 800-XXX-XXXX

11/11/99

XYZ Corporation, Inc.
Main Street
Anywhere, NY 10000

Attn.: Accounts Payable

Re: Account No. XY1000

Dear Sir/Madam:

The following invoice(s) is/are past due. Help us to continue our publishing work by remitting at your earliest possible convenience.

Date	Invoice	Amount	Payment	Credit	Balance	Due

*** Total ***

Thank you for your attention.

Sincerely,

Bruce Savage
Credit Manager

Figure 4. *Wilderness Studio collection letter for accounts with open items of forty days.*

10. Image Creation and Design

At Wilderness Studio we produce note cards and fine art graphic posters. This means posters that are sold as art. A poster is a well designed combination of text and image. The origin of the form stems from advertising, either of a product or an art exhibit. Although in recent times we have seen a somewhat looser sense of the fine art graphic poster, there is no doubt that it contains graphics as well as image. The graphics must be appropriate and add to, rather than detract from, the imagery. In other words, the total package must work. It should be remembered that the poster is to be marketed as art. I feel that it is helpful in this respect to remember that one of the origins of the form was the exhibition poster, designed to promote a gallery or museum show of an artist. Also, note that a high proportion of the profit in the art poster industry is in the framing. Therefore, it is important to design an image which can be framed in various ways and which high quality frame shops will like.

Notecards and greeting cards are produced in "flats", that is, more than one up on the printing sheet with the multiple images stripped together. We are currently running cards thirteen up. Roughly speaking, the cost of running a flat of cards is about the same as running one poster.

Since a poster is a great deal more expensive to produce than a card, we have sometimes looked to the sales of a specific image as a card in order to see if we should make a poster from it.

There is an image of mine I really like. It depicts two tombstones. An arm comes out of each tombstone and shakes the hand of the other one. As a card, this image has done very well for us. I decided to make a poster out of it and put the caption "True Love is Eternal" as the graphics on the poster. As a poster, this image was disastrous. We sold very few of them. It is our worst selling poster, and perhaps one of the worst selling posters of all times. Why did this image work as a card and not as a poster? What moral is to be learned from the sad story of "Eternal Love"?

Most narrowly, people do not wish to be reminded of death. While they will send a card that refers to death in certain contexts or as a joke, they will not frame Death and put it on their walls. The image was just not *appropriate* as a poster. Appropriateness is a truly key concept in product design and creation. Try to objectively identify the reasons people would (and would *not*) buy your product. Be objective, and do not allow yourself to be swayed by your enthusiasm for your own imagery. This is a good area to try to get informed feedback. It might be a good idea to bring your imagery to a workshop. As artists, our works are our children, and who can be really objective about the success or failure of their offspring? It is my firm belief that the most important skill an artist, photographer or publisher can have is the ability to edit creative work effectively.

Try to keep firmly in mind the consumer context of the product. Cards, even those without captions, are used to send messages or for occasions. "Happy Birthday", "Merry Christmas", and "I love you" are good examples. How many other themes or occasions can you identify? There will always be a market for interesting images illustrating these, or containing cats or humor. One thing I have observed about many greeting cards is a subtext of hostility or aggression. Speculation is possible about the cause of this—perhaps the sender of a "message" card who feels the need to mail it rather than say it is often unconsciously angry—but it is a fact of paper product life. Images which mask this kind of subtext with surface humor will often succeed as cards, cf. my "Eternal Love" image discussed above. Another example of the "hostile" card is all the birthday cards with jokes about the recipient's age.

Art posters are rather different. My successful posters represent a fantasy, a place that people can escape to, a place they would like to be. They must also be perceived as art.

Expect that even at best your first attempt will not totally succeed. An acquaintance of mine, an architect, designed a series of die cut cards in the shape of Victorian houses. These cards were intricately and beautifully made, but his card company didn't really happen until the next series, which were die cut images of animals.

Compile a collection of well designed things. In particular, find ten that are close to the product you would like to create. Make a list of the things you like about these ten, paying particular attention to design elements.

Consider tying your product to a cause in which you believe or a current popular mood, either through choice of imagery or donation of a percentage to a charity (the Sierra Club and Unicef are two of the best known beneficial recipients of paper product marketing strategies of this kind).

It might be worth your while to hire a consultant who is knowledgeable about the poster or card industry and/or to work with a good designer. Anyone who can save you from wasting time and money is worth the charge.

Production and design are intertwined in a complicated way in that production choices compel design solutions and design decisions make production choices. As noted in Section 13, "Production", someone *must* oversee the production process and approve the product as it is printed. If this is not you, it will probably be your designer.

How do you find a good designer? Eleanor Caponigro suggests asking who designed products or pieces you admire. Caponigro notes that you should not expect free advice from professionals. By the time she has estimated a job, and has gotten a printer to estimate on it, she figures about $1000 of professional time has been spent. Along with other top designers of art posters, she feels that the effort of design should stay in the background. If you notice the design first, or if it detracts from the art work, it is not good. Also, when you go to established designers, you are going to them for their look. Within reason, expect them to do it their way. If you are going to fight them about this, do not hire them in the first place. After all, design is their expertise.

Consideration should be given to the creation of a uniform look for the product line. This means that some kind of standard template for the information that will go on the piece should be developed. For example, the backs of most cards will always need to have the trade name of the company in big type (e.g., "Wilderness Studio"), title of the card (if appropriate), credit line to the photographer or artist, copyright notice, address, product code and price. Larger mass market card lines will also want to include a bar code. This information can be designed once, with typeface, position and size specified. In addition to the obvious advantage of saving money by not having to reinvent the design each time, this will also help to create consumer awareness of your product line, look and trade name.

11. Market Positioning

My company Wilderness Studio started publishing through what in retrospect seems like a total fluke. In 1980 I had an exhibit of my photographs at Arras Gallery on 57th Street in New York. *American Photographer* magazine did a review of the show and reproduced my "Water Lilies" poster which had been published by Modernart Editions. In his otherwise mixed review of the exhibit Owen Edwards wrote regarding the poster: "Here is a photograph of nature with a beauty rooted not in the overworked style of 'nature photography' but in the painting of Monet, or the subtle, evocative spaces of antique Japanese screens."

At the end of the year the magazine produced a packet of cards as a gift to advertisers which included this image. They were happy to give me the overruns of the cards. I took the overruns around to my local card stores and discovered they were eager to buy them. Using the same production sources that *American Photographer* had, I then produced a "flat" of ten postcards. Very quickly I discovered that I couldn't spend my time going from card store to card store, so I found a sales rep for New York City by asking buyers at card stores whom they liked to buy from and who they thought would be a good rep for my product. I got friendly with this sales rep, and he connected me with a few others in different parts of the country. The rest, as they say, is history. One useful reference tool for locating sales reps is *The Rep Directory* published by Lin Berla Enterprises (New York, 1987, unfortunately now out of print). Of course, first you have to find this book (try business libraries) which originally cost about $160 and listed gift, stationery, tabletop and housewares manufacturers' representatives in the United States categorized geographically and by the kind of product they carry. Be cautioned: independent manufacturers reps are a peripatetic lot, and this information gets old very quickly. Trade shows are perhaps the best place to find professional sales reps. Most good reps attend the shows, and some of the shows have bulletin boards that list reps who want product and places to advertise for reps. If you are exhibiting a quality product, reps will come to you at the trade shows. Finally, word of mouth from other card companies works well since most reps will not carry competitive lines in any case. Your direct competitors will be cautious about giving you information, but this does not matter because if they truly are direct competitors, you should not be sharing sales reps.

While it would be my hope that any venture you undertake is done with a bit more research on your part than was done on mine, there is a technique to be learned from what I did. It is a good idea to create a mock up of your product as close as possible to what it will really be like. I was fortunate enough to have had this done for me by *American Photographer* for reasons of their own. Take the mock up and show it to as many buyers as will talk to you. See if they will buy this product. Will they make some commitment to you before it is produced? Listen closely to any comments they may have. This information is very valuable. Also, mock-up in hand, seek out distributors and sales reps if appropriate. These people will actually be selling your proposed product. Their input and enthusiasm are crucial, and by involving them in the planning stage, they may be more motivated to actually carry your product once it really exists.

For your own sake, although this could also become an important part of your business plan, take the time to generate a written marketing plan. Putting it down in words will help you clarify and focus.

Spend a great deal of time in the kind of stores that you hope will sell your product. Become familiar with the different brands and how they are distinctive. Try to create a product that is not a copy or "knock-off" of something already on the market. On the other hand, if there is nothing already there even remotely like yours, why not? It is difficult enough to create a distinctive line within an existing sales niche or category. It is almost impossible to create the niche itself unless you have the marketing power of a large corporation behind you. Remember: Not only consumers must like your product. The environment of the industry in which you are operating must be favorable to your venture. For example, everyone acknowledges that the card business is almost insatiable in its demand for new material. A major factor in this is that card store buyers, who are very visual people, get bored at looking at the same merchandise repeatedly, however well it sells to their customers.

Do pay special attention to the pricing and production values of competitive products. Yours must be comparable.

One approach that has worked with cards is to design a line around a specific geographic area with either tourist or local (or both) purchasing potential. A case in point is Alan Batt's extremely successful "Piece of the Rainbow" which features Alan's rather eccentric and highly humorous New York photography on captioned greeting cards. Obviously, a high percentage of sales for this line is going to come from the New York area. Alan, who is an articulate and skillful salesperson, has the best possible New York rep: himself. The moral is that if you do have a product with primarily one geographic market, it is much more feasible to sell it yourself. (On a slightly digressive note, it is often the case that the creator of a product can sell it better than anyone else even though this may be an undesirable or non cost effective way to use his time. Beyond more motivation and familiarity with the product, I have found that with a professional product with a national reputation, buyers simply feel guilty about saying, "No," when the artist walks in the door.)

Posters can also be geographically targeted, particularly lower priced tourist posters. Fine art posters, however, while they may have a geographic hook, such as my "New York, New York" or "Denali, the Great One, Alaska", must also have a general appeal in order to be successful. This is because the market for wall art (posters) is "shallower" than for cards or tourist oriented products. There are only so many walls in a given area. Also, as they are bulkier and more fragile, tourists cannot as easily buy posters (as opposed to cards which are a cliche tourist item).

Cards are meant to convey a message such as "Hello, thinking of you!" or "Happy Birthday." More than half the greeting cards sold in the United States are for Christmas or related seasonal use. "Happy Birthday" accounts for the lion's share of the remaining half with Valentine's Day and other card-appropriate holidays filling in most of the balance of sales. Anyone building a card line needs to understand this and act accordingly.

"Line Building" is a very important concept which involves two important techniques. One is, "if something works, do more of it." The trick here is to try to figure out the essence of the success of the product. What about my "Dance of Spring" poster makes it sell? Is it the delicate pastel image in pinks and white showing a creek which could be anywhere surrounded by the buds of early spring? Is it the text running along the bottom of the poster which states in a light grey italic typeface "The Dance of Spring is the Dance of Life"? Is it the reference to the season? Whatever it is, try to uncover the formula and present buyers with other related options. (You can be sure that if the formula can be copied someone else will.) Two, "cover the board." If there are obvious functional product slots, make sure you have them filled. If you are creating a line of holiday related cards, be sure that there are Valentine's Day cards as well as Christmas cards in your product mix.

What are the best promotional materials to be going with your line, and what should you be telling buyers? As one well known buyer puts it, this is an area where less is definitely more. Assume that buyers are knowledgeable, and let them bring out facts via questioning. Be concise and professional. Don't let your ego get involved in interactions with buyers. Don't get involved in competitions as to who is busier or more knowledgeable, and don't look for stroking. Regard selling to buyers as an educational process for them and pass on to them the information you would like them to convey to their customers. This certainly applies to a wholesale business such as posters as well as to a business in which you are selling directly to retailers. Tell your distributors what they should be telling their retailers. Never apologize for the product or point out things that could be done better.

Be aware that marketing is not the same as selling. Marketing is the broader picture where a single sale does not matter that much. Marketing is the strategy for creating the possibility of sales; it is not the actual closing of sales. Your sales reps or distributors may only be able to focus on their own interests in making individual sales, for example, the need for new product. It is your job as Director of Marketing to see the broader view.

Finally, "a thing of beauty is a joy forever". To the extent that you can bring joy, light and happiness to those who see, touch or buy your product, everything else will fall into place. We get most when we give.

12. Financing

Being independently wealthy (or simply having the cash) is the easiest way of financing a start-up business venture. Failing this, you might look to the equity in your home, your life savings, or the advances available on your MasterCard. A minimum investment to produce anything via offset would probably be at least $10,000. Las Vegas is less risky. Unless you have other property to use as collateral, banks will not lend money to an emerging paper goods company. They will not regard your inventory as security because they cannot dispose of it should they have to foreclose. Generally, banks require two escape routes: (1) a demonstration that the business will generate income to service and amortize (repay) the loan, and (2) collateral as security for the loan so that in case the business does not generate the income necessary to repay the loan the bank can sell the collateral and cover itself. You will want to know that inventory, unless it happens to be gold bullion, generally does not meet the second condition.

Venture capitalists will generally be seeking a high tech or "sexy" industry and, in any case, will want a substantial percentage of equity and profits and a way to cash out in the foreseeable future in exchange for their stake.

I have heard that the S.B.A. and state and local development agencies represent a possible source of capital and help; however, my own personal experience with this sort of bureaucracy has not been good.

Knowing these facts of life will save you valuable time, what avenues beyond your personal resources are available?

A well thought out business plan is an absolutely essential first step. This has virtues beyond simply helping you sell your request for funding. It will help you focus on areas that you might not otherwise have been clear about.

Depending on whom you intend to present it to, it need not be formal. Perhaps you should get help creating the plan. There are several excellent books on how to write a business plan. The act of creating the plan will force you to think things out. The plan will also be a valuable tool when you go to potential sponsors. Try to project expenses and income for at least three years. Be hard nosed and realistic.

What other possible sources of financing are there? You might consider friends and people interested in your work. Along this line, there is also the possibility of organizations who would like to have their name on your printed piece for public relations reasons. These might include suppliers, art galleries, travel destinations, and charitable causes.

Suppliers such as printers may be a possible source of help, either directly or through the extension of trade credit. After all, they have an interest in encouraging new business as well as in having their name on a sample of fine printing. However, financing a business with trade credit takes strong guts. You might well find yourself three, six or nine months down the road with large printing bills and no money to pay them. This approach may not be fair to the suppliers and might jeopardize your business, even if it is successful, by leaving you without trade suppliers who are willing to work with you. Printers are wary of self-publishers of cards, books and posters because a very substantial part of their default losses come from this kind of customer.

Art galleries that you are affiliated with have a strong interest in visual self-promotion and image creation. They also have art world connections and a built-in market for the sale of posters and cards. Booster organizations for a travel destination, for example the Chamber of Commerce, possibly have a complementary interest to yours in getting gorgeous images of their city or scenery in distribution.

Your sales represent another source of income and therefore financing. It is sometimes possible to take orders for product before the product has been printed. The "paper" thus created can be sold to a commercial factor if the account is credit worthy for about 60% of its face value up front. However, factors will more typically expect you to complete delivery satisfactorily before they pay you, so this means that you can probably not expect your 60% until several months after printing, even if all goes very well. Drawbacks here include the expense (the factor will take 10-15% for financing an invoice that is nominally due in 30 days) and paperwork (the factor will insist on a UCC filing on your receivables). It is to be noted that banks will finance receivables only when the volume is substantial (e.g. constant open invoices of more than $50,000) and the accounts blue chip. A more advantageous approach, if you can make if fly, is to offer potential customers a substantial discount for cash in advance pre-publication orders.

The discussion above is primarily based on what might be thought of as a left-brained analytic approach to financing, where the key question is, How do we raise a lump sum to cover production of inventory? I think of this as the "my uncle is the CEO of Citibank" approach. One problem with financing a self-publishing business this way is that it is too easy. All too often, people who have been able to raise money this way do not face the realities of marketing and profitability. And, if the venture goes down the tubes, they will not starve but rather move on to the next thing. At a certain point in the history of a publishing venture one will probably need a large infusion of outside capital to move from the plateau of initial success to the plateau of long term institutional existence. However, in the beginning, my personal feeling is that it is better to bootstrap, think small and be market driven. Go with the flow. A bootstrapping right-brained operation can afford only one or two mistakes before it is out of business. Each product it creates must have a market niche and an acceptable margin of profitability. The discipline of having to be careful is worthwhile.

As the discussion above indicates, I am basically a believer in an organic approach. A case in point is the successful Stationery Sounds, founded by husband and wife team John and Bonnie Reed. Bonnie had a background in fashion design, art history and arts administration; John was a musician. Between performances of a Broadway show John created musical card designs to help pass the time. They published these cards, which were funny line drawn cartoons related to music, on an ad hoc basis. The cards did sufficiently well to encourage them to learn about the card business and printing and to develop a national sales network. The next step involved meeting a famous artist and publishing his work in a series of beautiful four color cards. After this, Bonnie persuaded a friend of hers who was painting lush florals in her attic to let Stationery Sounds publish a series of cards. Seeing the quality work Stationery Sounds was producing, other artists started coming to them.

Bonnie is always looking for something new and for creative ways of publishing. She likes working co-operatively with artists. She notes that an alternative card company must be very good to compete today. "Costs of operating and production are higher than people realize. Remember that every time you buy a greeting card it originally came from a tree. Consider all the processes between the raw tree and the final product at the store where it is retailing for $1.50." Her answer? She pays special attention to production values. "Buyers notice quality printing." She uses her intelligence and imagination, schemes, and works with other companies and artists.

She views competitors not as enemies but as possible allies. "As soon as I find someone paranoid I don't talk to him."

There is also the question of the form of your business organization. Should you operate as a sole proprietorship, a partnership, or a corporation? If you have a partner, by all means enter into a formal partnership agreement. If you are operating as a sole proprietor or a partnership, by all means file a d/b/a (doing business as) form with your business name. In any case, as a wholesale business you should obtain a Certificate of Authority to collect sales tax. The number on this form is your "Resale Number".

The question of whether to form a corporation is one that you may need competent professional advice about. Certainly, the record keeping and filing requirements for a corporation are more complicated, and there are, initial costs involved as well as annual minimum corporate taxes even in the absence of income. Also, the benefits of limited corporate liability are often exaggerated. For one thing, any financing institution will probably require a personal guarantee. And many plaintiffs suing your corporation will also name you personally as a defendant.

On the plus side, operating as a corporation does provide some personal insulation which is a benefit if you have substantial personal resources and if the business meets disaster. Also, a corporate structure makes it easier to formally allocate equity interests and harder to merge personal and company monies. It may also help create the image of size and stability. Finally, there is substantially more room for maneuvering items such as compensation and withholding to your personal benefit.

Follow business formalities. Keep good records, file papers in a timely fashion and pay your taxes. Nothing can get you out of business faster than the IRS, and an IRS judgment can follow you even after a receivership. Until and unless you are competent to pursue such matters yourself, get a good accountant. Even if your business cannot afford the ongoing costs of expert accounting help, pay somebody good to help you get set up. This way you will have someone to call on an as-needed basis. Read Section 9 on "Automating the Office" and consider taking some courses in accounting and/or computers. Get good business advice. Think big but be prepared for the worst. Good luck!

13. Production

Production consists of everything beyond the conception phase to the actual physical manufacture of the product. This includes connecting the correct text material with the correct image, proofing text, ordering type, creating a mechanical, separating art, proofing the separations, creating a printer's blue print, running the material on press and finishing and packaging the product. There are various possible intermediate steps and other ways of doing it, but this is the basic gist. In other words, production is a mine field, an arena in which all participants are constantly watching for Murphy's Law in action.

Established publishers have important employees as Production Managers. They oversee the process outlined above and go on press runs to okay color and everything else. Perhaps you will be working with a designer who can do this for you. But most likely you will have to do it yourself which means getting involved with the printer and going on press.

A friend of mine once had a book of his published, of which he was rightly proud. He felt that the book was perfect. We bet him that on any page he chose we could find a typographic error. Thinking to out-fox us, he selected the title page. We found that his name was misspelled in the copyright notice. Try this yourself with published material and see how many mistakes you can find.

A small paper goods company had produced and distributed a very successful line of note cards of New York City. They started producing calendars, and the first year had a notable success. But the next year, January was inadvertently printed with 30 (not 31) days. The product was shipped to stores before anyone noticed, and, in fact, was only called to anyone's attention by an irate customer whose birthday fell on January 31. All the product had to be recalled, money refunded, and the mistake drove this company out of business.

The goal is to produce your product with absolutely no mistakes.

There are many good books on production. For references to some, please see Appendix I: Resources: 1. Books.

Printing involves a complex interaction among technology, people and aesthetics. It is also a commercial process in which some compromise is inevitable. Press time is a very expensive commodity. With this as background, please understand that most printers are not very enthusiastic about input from lay people. The printing industry is structured so that the least expensive way to execute a project is generally to contract out each part to a so-called "trade shop". Printing brokers are the people who do this and serve as barriers between the trade printing industry and the public. If you go instead to a full service printer, a salesperson will generally perform the function of the broker. Therefore, you can cut out the printing broker, and his commission, if you are willing to go directly to trade suppliers and if they are willing to work with you. The characteristics of each printing shop are different, but be clear that the level of technology employed is not the most important factor. Work done with care on old two color presses will probably be better than work churned out on modern fully computerized six color presses. The most essential ingredient is a willingness to care. The printer must realize that an object like an art poster is *art* and will stand or fall on the quality with which it is produced unlike, with all due respect, annual reports, or advertising brochures, which, while they may be produced with great quality, are not intended to go on walls and be studied *ad infinitum*. Also, a fancy annual report or brochure is not produced within the economic constraints of the creation of a product intended for resale, and cost is not very important. Beware of any printer who specializes in fancy annual reports and advertising brochures and look for a printer who is willing to truly consider your project the joint creation of a work of art.

What follows is a brief description of the production process which assumes that you will be using a sheet fed press.

First, you need to know roughly what you are doing. It doesn't matter whether your idea is sketched on the back of a menu or done formally, but you need to have and be able to communicate a good sense of what your product will look like. This includes such things as kind and weight of paper ("stock"), finish (pieces may be laminated or varnished) and colors. One way to do this is to bring in product similar in production values to what you want to end up with.

Generally, design information is conveyed to the printer via a "mechanical" which is literally a board or a piece of paper with the exact size of the finished piece indicated on it. There are basically three elements to a mechanical: (1) cropping indications, usually via photostat or xerox to size, for any visual imagery; (2) black and white exact reproductions of type ready to be photographed and incorporated into printing plates; and (3) instructions about things that are not otherwise clear and non-process ("PMS") colors.

These days anything with extensive text should for reasons of economy and control be set on your PC (using either a desk top publishing package or Wordperfect version 5.0 or later) with the resulting disk processed via a linotype service bureau. A caveat: this process is not necessarily as straight forward as it sounds. Please be sure you know what you are doing and have discussed it with someone experienced before attempting.

However, with cards and posters, because of both the lack of quantity of text and the size of type (termed "display faces") setting type the old-fashioned way through a high quality typositor shop is economically feasible.

The mechanical should be delivered along with the art work to the separator (or printer if he is to be responsible for the separations). These professionals (or your designer if you are working with one) should be able to give you reliable input at an early stage as to the technical reproducibility of your original. Generally, chromes work better than reflected art. Look for sharp, clean originals.

Please understand the distinction between "process" color and non-process color. "Process" color is what printers use to make the optical illusion of color by breaking the art down into the primary colors (the convention is Red, Yellow, Blue and Black, hence the term "four color process"). An analogy that may be helpful here is to consider a musical choir. We have broken down the music into parts, soprano, bass, etc.; yet the audience hears the parts come together in one blended whole. In theory, every color we perceive can be made through the four color process. For many reasons, however, it is often necessary to add further non-process colors that are mixed directly from ink. For example, lettering on a white background will probably have to be done with an additional color if it is to appear sharp in the final piece. The most commonly used system for specifying non-process colors is the Pantone PMS system. Bear in mind that this system cannot reproduce all colors and that it represents a starting point.

You will need a camera ready mechanical. The mechanical consists of type which is ready to be shot for reproduction together with an "fpo" (for position only) photostat to indicate positioning of the imagery and instructions to the printer. Crucial here is the percentage magnification of the art work. If you do not have the skills to do this yourself, you will need to hire a good mechanical artist or designer. This person can probably also help you with ordering ("specing") type.

Your art work needs to be separated so that plates can be made for the four color process. If your original art is "transparent", i.e. a slide, the separation can be made directly from this, although it might be a wise procedure to have a very high quality duplicate made first, or even to use the dupe for reproduction. If your original is "reflected art", such as a painting, you will first have to photograph the art work to create a transparency (although it is sometimes possible to put flexible reflected copy on a scanning drum and shoot it directly). Go to a reputable company that specializes in the photography of art work and get a 4"x5" or larger chrome.

You will be presented with a proof of some kind from the separation. There are a number of different proofing systems, but the key distinction to bear in mind is between a press proof, where "progressive" printing has actually been made on a small "proving" press, and synthetic proofs generated on some kind of plastic laminate film. Chromalins and color keys are proprietary terms for separations of the latter sort. Press proofs, of course, will give you a better idea of what you might actually expect on your real press run; however, they are a quite expensive way to go and realistically unnecessary once you have some experience with the other systems and how they juxtapose from plastic to paper.

You should also be shown a blueprint by the printer which shows everything as it will actually be positioned on the job. Check this carefully.

Production in general and the printing run in particular are not exact sciences. Experience will be the best teacher. Working well with the people on press, both blue collar and executives, is crucial. Do not hesitate to reject initial versions and to stand up for what your eye tells you is right. However, these people are professionals who do their best and are expert in what is possible. Let them tell you what the options are, but do, not expect the impossible. Be particularly watchful for small hickeys, dots and dust. If you license an image to an outside publishing company, actively participate in the production process if your publisher will allow it and go on the press OK.

The proof may be acceptable (unlikely the first time around) as it is, or it may need a series of corrections. Once you have an acceptable proof, select a suitable stock, approve blueprints, and reach agreement with your printer, you will be ready to set a press date. Again, it is not a wise idea to leave final approval of press runs to the printer for the printer's sake as well as your own. Since compromise will be involved, make it your compromise.

Any printer who is reluctant to have you and/or your designer on press should be firmly avoided.

Assuming all goes well on press, you will have to make arrangements to finish, pack and ship the product to your warehouse (or living room, as the case may be).

14. Fulfillment

Fulfillment means packing and shipping orders. There are four basic patterns for handling this: (1) Do it yourself on an ad hoc basis, using a basement, spare room or living room and possibly hiring part time help; (2) Use a fulfillment warehouse; (3) Join forces with one or two other (hopefully non-competitive) small publishing businesses; (4) Establish your own modern warehousing facility. The last is the only option likely to be fully satisfying; however, it is, of course, beyond the domain of possibility for most small businesses.

Doing it yourself has the advantage of being the least expensive choice. At least initially, it is educational. The disadvantages are that you lack the systems, expertise and, possibly, the space. Also, packing is obviously not a good long term investment of your time. This means not only will you have to turn your living or studio space into a warehouse, but you will also have to supervise manual labor in your space. From a psychological point of view, the combination of these things can be such a turn off that you may find yourself saying, "Oh no! Not another order. Please, no. Anything but more packing!" Obviously this is not the right frame of mind in which to be creating marketing and selling strategies.

Using a fulfillment warehouse has the advantage of having professionals handle everything. They know about packaging and have working relationships with the shippers. You do not need to see the actual inventory. If you need special post-production packing, such as boxing card sets, or shrink wrapping, they can handle this for you. The main disadvantage is the expense, which will be expressed both as a monthly rent and as a per order handling charge. This can be so high as to seriously jeopardize the profitability of the product. However, it is a real expense, even if, when doing it yourself, you are probably not as aware of it.

Another disadvantage of the fulfillment house is that you have to deal with the sometimes sluggish bureaucracy of that company. This may cause you to have to generate more paperwork, and you may not be able to ship certain kinds of orders. (For example, the fee charged for processing C.O.D. paperwork may make it impractical to ship small orders C.O.D.) You also may not be able to ship as quickly as if you were doing it yourself. The possibility of theft or loss at the warehouse is another potential problem. Finally, the fulfillment house has your inventory and is in a position to shut you down if the relationship goes sour.

Finding other small companies to work with sounds like a good idea. In practice, the difficulty lies in finding companies who are creating a product close enough to yours so that the fulfillment issues are similar yet non-competitive enough so that you can work together without fearing sabotage or theft of clients. Also, who will do the actual work of managing the warehouse? If they do, why should they really be committed to you? If you do, are you really ready to go into the business of managing a warehouse? In short, the difficulties are basically those of fit and relationship. I do, however, know of one or two situations where this has worked. For example, an art poster company and a sports poster company where the sports company also has a wholesale framing operation which is not operating at capacity.

Whichever way you choose to go, some things will remain constant. Packages that are professional both in functionality and appearance are a must. After all, the container your client gets your product in is the context, stage and frame in which your product is viewed. Concise and legible accompanying paperwork, containing customer purchase order number and your invoice number is a necessity. Damages will be a constant ongoing expense and headache in the art poster business and will require a great deal of attention. Cards will require packing with envelopes either for gift boxing or for wholesaling in dozens. And new paper goods products will need imaginative packaging designs.

15. Collections

The first thing to note about collections is that this is an area to which every wholesale business needs to give careful attention.

Keep track of accounts receivable. Generate aging of receivables for your own information at least twice a month and flag potential problems. Send out statements to all accounts with open balances regularly (once a month) and past due notices in a timely fashion to accounts that are past due.

Of course, this is an area in which prevention is the best cure. Take the best precautions you can about whom you sell to and use horse sense. A C.O.D. (cash on delivery) requirement on initial orders is reasonable (although, in fact, it will not make good business sense to be rigid about this as there are some absolutely blue chip customers who will not work this way). Do get bank and trade credit references, and follow up on them before giving a client open account status. The conventional wisdom is that most losses come from sole proprietorships, which is one of the reasons why discussion of how not to appear to be a sole proprietor does appear elsewhere in this book. However, do bear this in mind when making credit granting decisions.

Despite precautions, every business is bound to have at least some problems and losses. *Statistically, the longer an account is past due the less likely it ever is to pay.* If you are considering the theory of collections, the last sentence should be underlined as it is the most important single thing to know. The implication is that it makes sense to take assertive action as soon as possible. Assuming you are basically selling on a Net 30 Day basis. This means the first phone call should be made at around 40 days. A caveat here: it is obviously not worth the expense (and time) of more than a very few calls across the continent in an attempt to collect small amounts. (The minimum wholesale card order varies, but $50.00 is not unusual.) Thus, from a card publisher's point of view, the bottom line may be that there is no practical way to collect outside of his geographic area.

Returning to the first phone call, the problem here is that we are reluctant to pick up the phone and disturb our clients when for all we know "the check is in the mail". The best advice is to rely on the principle underlined above and just do it. The truth is that there is really no cost effective way to collect from a client who simply will not pay unless huge sums of money are involved, and even then it's not a sure thing considering receivership statutes, other loopholes, and the cost of hiring effective legal help. The things we have going for us are: (1) the fairly widespread desire to do business in an ethical way; (2) a reluctance to cheat artists; (3) the difficulty in conducting business, particularly retail business, while being dunned; and (4) the most important factor, namely the desire of the client to continue to do business with you and to carry your product.

I suggest that you be tough about granting credit and tough about shipping subsequent orders when earlier ones remain unpaid. The easiest way for this to not become a problem is by it not starting out as one. When payment is late, the sooner you get on it, the better. Understand the only four leverage points you have as listed above. There is little point in making threats you won't be able to follow through on. Your clients are not fools. Use courtesy, persistence and guilt.

16. Coping With Cash Flow Problems

This section covers an unpleasant topic, namely how to manage your publishing business which is in trouble in such a way that it will recover. Obviously, no one wants to manage or own a business that is in trouble. By "in trouble" and "in crisis" we specifically mean financial and cash flow problems, although other kinds of difficulties are certainly possible, and, indeed, sometimes related. Certainly, only general observations are possible here, and I would urge the reader to get expert help as needed. Finally, I would like to note that this is an area in which having a positive outlook is both essential and difficult, difficult because this society tends to equate personal value with net worth and because your creditors will attempt to use guilt to collect from you. Try to remember that you are a good and important person independent of how much money you have in the bank, and independent of the success or failure of your business. Also, as an artist you are a good person trying to do creative service and to give birth to a good product, in a monotonous world. Be stubborn!

At a certain point, analogies to amputation will come to mind, with comparable questions involved: What are the chances that the limb (business) can be saved? Does it make sense to invest further time, energy or money? Obviously, recovery of the business is what we want, and this section will consider some aspects of recovery. However, without short term survival we cannot even start dealing with long term recovery. We will focus on short term survival strategies, and on how to make the decision to amputate. There are possibly both business and emotional reasons for sticking with a business that is not doing so well. To quote Napoleon Hill, "A quitter never wins—and a winner never quits." However, the amputation metaphor is a good one: better to amputate the gangrenous limb than lose the patient. The patient is your entire financial picture, and presumably the business that is in trouble is only one aspect of this picture, bringing up an important point: to every extent possible, personal finances should be (a) clearly conceptualized as separate from the business;

and (b) when possible disentangled from the business (note that this is not the same as (a)). Also, consideration of the amputation metaphor occurs again in considering the problems we will be attempting to solve. At what point does it make sense to write off credit cards, credit lines, indebtedness, and trade credit? When do we consider some form of bankruptcy? Filing Chapter 7 or Chapter 11, personally and/or for the business, can be a viable option. Even the threat of doing so may result in positive renegotiation of payment terms. However, further analysis of receivership is beyond the scope of this discussion; please seek expert advice.

As noted above, a positive attitude during the stressful times that the owner or manager of the small publishing business in crisis will be experiencing is very important. One constructive way to look at things is try to experience all events around the business crisis as a learning experience, one that will have benefits once the business has recovered. Another mental attitude that we need to be clear about up front is that survival of the business in grave financial distress is not a matter for boy scouts to handle. Survival, the life and death survival, of the business is at stake, and if we are committed to it, we must overcome a number of scruples.

First, evaluate whether the business is worth saving. Even without it, you have your other life, and your work as an artist. Is there a viable chance of recovery sufficient to justify the additional investment of time and money? Is the difficulty you are experiencing a short term blip or a long term fundamental problem?

If we are resolved to save the publishing operation, we must do so in a steadfast spirit, with no shame, and be resolved to overcome all obstacles.

Bills and debts will need to be placed in several categories. At the top of the list comes the phone bill, which you must pay to stay in business. There are probably a very few other items which you must keep current. Next come those items which there is some leeway about but basically you must maintain. In this category would fall rent and vital trade suppliers. The next group would be secured debts. In the short run there are no negative consequences to not paying these kinds of bills (e.g. leases on equipment) except nasty phone calls and letters. In the long run, repossession may be a possibility. The last category are bills which you can avoid with relative impunity, such as unsecured loans and trade suppliers whose services you no longer need or who can be easily replaced.

Stop paying bills. Don't pay anything you don't have to pay. Negotiate delayed payment plans with key suppliers. Cut out any non-essential expenses. Is there staff you can let go, or advertising you can terminate? Consider and come up with some creative schemes for decreasing expenses. Cut out any fat.

At the same time, maximize cash flow. Put as much pressure as you can on your customers to pay you quickly (see Section 15, "Collections"). Consider giving them a discount for cash payment or pre-payment. Consider factoring your receivables. Go out and sell, sell, sell!

While engineering short term survival, don't ignore the long term picture. What are the reasons for the crisis, and what will turn it around? Consider finding an outside source of financing (See Section 12). Is there an essential problem with the product, or with its marketing, and, if so, what can be done to correct it? Is the product, as priced, sufficiently profitable? Using what you have learned about publishing your work, can you introduce a new product that will sell like gangbusters? Generate a year's projected month by month income and expenses chart. Try faith and prayer. Get help when you need it: consider some form of support group such as Debtors Anonymous. If necessary, get good legal advice and consult with industry experts. Remember that those who threaten you the loudest (assuming you haven't been financing your business with the help of the baseball bat and knees crowd) generally have the least actual power.

17. Staying a Creative Artist

Artists have to work twice as hard as anyone else. Like everybody, they have to make a living. They also have to stay creative. The jobs don't necessarily overlap. It may take many years for even a productive and talented artist to realize substantial income from his work.

In our context, the other job might be self-publishing. Self-publishing can quickly become publishing which can involve things very far from art such as dealing with banks, shippers and warehouses.

There is no formula for staying creative as an artist. It is a little like the search for the fountain of youth. But, clearly, one thing that is essential is to plan quality time for artistic creation. This can seem difficult to justify because in real dollar terms it may feel non-productive. However, without adequate time to create there will be nothing.

It is also important to attempt to disengage one's need for ego gratification from one's sales. (By the way, this is true for the one of a kind painter with discerning patrons as well.) The public that buys the work may or may not be responding to profound artistic impulses; indeed, it is arguably not their business to respond to such. I have reached the point where, as agent for myself, I feel, "I don't care what you call it, just pay me for it." But when you are wearing the hat of artist, you need to insulate yourself from issues of sales. Otherwise, gradually and step by step, you will begin the long slide into caring about the positive feedback you are getting via sales and producing more of the same to get the same positive feedback. Wear two hats: business person representing yourself as artist and artist. As business person you just want the sales; you could care less what they say. As artist, satisfy yourself. If you get compliments and love in addition to money and self-satisfaction, smile and gracefully acknowledge it, but do not take it too seriously or let it go to your head.

Enjoy what you do. Take pride and pleasure in your work when it is well done. Don't ever let yourself get bored. If you get bored, do something else for a while.

Accept that creativity goes in cycles. At different times you will be into doing different things, and this is as it should be. I have been variously obsessed with painting, photography, writing, publishing and computers. Obviously I don't work full time in each of these areas simultaneously. Yet, each time I have dropped and resumed a creative activity it has been at a higher level. And the work in different areas impacts synergistically in ways I can't even imagine as I am doing it.

Also, use the time in which you cannot be artistically productive to take good care of yourself physically, emotionally and spiritually.

Set an artificial cap on your working day as a publisher. Let it be one hour a day or ten, but whatever it is, make it all right to be a puttering artist after your working day as a publisher is done.

Finally, it is best to think of oneself as a channel. I try to think of myself as a vessel for the expression of my art which itself comes from a higher power and a different plane. Whatever the literal truth of this, it works as a behavioral model. If I am only a channel, I am not responsible for the quality of the result and need not fear success or failure. I am responsible only for doing the best I can. This way of thinking works for me.

18. Conclusion

You are a winner as an artist and self-publisher if you:

- ☐ Become clear about your intentions as an artist and publisher;
- ☐ Separate the business and creative functions of your enterprise and perform each with the appropriate state of mind;
- ☐ Approach your business and art with a spiritually positive attitude;
- ☐ Create a detailed business plan in writing;
- ☐ License imagery to outside publishers and learn from their production process and marketing efforts;
- ☐ Automate, delegate or sub-contract routine tasks;
- ☐ Create and work with wonderful imagery;
- ☐ Use impeccable design and care about what you do;
- ☐ Have fun while you do it;
- ☐ Price and market your product appropriately;
- ☐ Finance your business in a sober, realistic and hard headed way;
- ☐ Plan to grow slowly;
- ☐ Learn all you can about production;
- ☐ Be extremely careful about production details;
- ☐ Be stubborn and persistent but open to new ideas;
- ☐ Stay a creative artist.

A quality product in the stores starts with quality thought at the very beginning. It is implemented with care, love, hard work, good design and impeccable decision making.

19. What About You?

I sincerely hope that this book has been informative and helpful to you. Let me hear from you. Please send comments, suggestions and reports on your continuing progress in this field to:

Harold Davis
c/o Wilderness Studio
299 Pavonia Ave.
Jersey City, NJ 07302.

APPENDIX I: RESOURCES

1. Books

Art Law: The Guide for Collectors, Investors, Dealers & Artists, Ralph E. Lerner and Judith Bresler, Practising Law Institute, New York, 1989. This fairly comprehensive work claims to encompass "all the legal ramifications involved in the creation, purchase, sale or transfer of a work of art." While the book is more geared to the area of original works of art rather than the reproduction thereof, it is generally helpful.

dBase III Handbook, George Tsu-der Chou, Que Corporation, Indianapolis, 1985.

The Design of Books, Adrian Wilson, Peregrine-Smith, Salt Lake City, 1974. An excellent introduction to book design; demonstrates the visual use of type without being overly intellectual.

The Encyclopedia of Small Business Resources, David E. Gumpert & Jeffrey A. Timmons, Harper & Row, 1984. An excellent compendium; particularly see the "Business Plan" section, pp 380-85.

Financial Accounting, 6th edition, Robert F. Meigs & Walter E. Meigs, McGraw-Hill, 1988.

Getting it Printed: How to Work with Printers and Graphic Arts Services to Assure Quality, Stay on Schedule, and Control Costs, Beach, Shepro, Russon, Coast to Coast Books, Portland, OR, 1986. An overview of the printing and production process from the point of view of the small book self-publisher.

Graphic Artists Guild Handbook: Pricing and Ethical Guidelines, Graphic Artists Guild, New York, 1984.

Graphics Master 4: Reference Guide and Workbook for the Design, Planning, Estimating and Production of Printing and Print Advertising, Dean Phillip Lem, Dean Lem Associates, Los Angeles, CA, 1988. Extremely comprehensive guide to paper, type, binding & finishing, etc. Dean Lem Associates can be reached at 800-562-2562.

Guide to Independent Art Reps, compiled by Caroline Myers Just, Art Business News, Stamford, CT, 1989.

How to Master the Art of Selling, Tom Hopkins, Warner Books, 1982. The best book on how to sell that I know. Highly recommended.

Mechanical Color Separation Skills for the Commercial Artist, Tom Cardamone, Van Nostrand Reinhold Company, New York, 1980. This book is fairly technical and does not cover process separations. However, it might give you some ideas.

Money is My Friend, Phil Laut, Vivation Publishing Co., P.O. Box 8269, Cincinnati, OH 45208, 513-321-4405. This self-published new age classic helps you to "make more money doing work that you love".

The Photo Marketing Handbook, Second revised edition, Jeff Cason and Peter Lawrence, Images Press, New York, 1990.

Photographer's Market {annual} and *Artist's Market* {annual}, Writer's Digest Books, Cincinnati, OH. Extensive listings and dubious accuracy.

Photographing for Publication: How to Create and Evaluate Photographs for Better Reproduction: A Guide for Photographers, Editors and Graphic Arts Professionals, Sanders & Norman, R.R. Bowker, New York, 1983.

Photography for the Art Market, Kathryn Marx, Amphoto, New York, 1988.

Pocket Pal: A Graphic Arts Production Handbook, International Paper Company, New York, undated. Classic paperback guide to the history, theory and practice of production and printing.

Preparing Art for Printing, Stone and Eckstein, Van Nostrand Reinhold, New York, 1965. Dated (e.g. pre-scanning technology only) but very thorough how-to book on pre-production.

Professional Business Practices in Photography, ASMP, American Society of Magazine Photographers, New York, 1986.

Stock Photography Handbook, ASMP, American Society of Magazine Photographers, New York, 1989. The bible of stock photography sales.

The Reproduction of Colour in Photography, Printing and Television, 4th ed., R.W.G. Hunt, Van Nostrand Reinhold Company, New York, 1987.

Think & Grow Rich, Napoleon Hill, Fawcett Crest, New York, 1960. Inspirational classic.

WordPerfect 5 Desktop Publishing in Style, Daniel Will-Harris, Peachpit Press, Berkeley, Ca., 1988.

A Writer's Guide to Book Publishing, Richard Balkin, Hawthorn/Dutton, New York, 1981.

2. Periodicals

Art Business News
60 Ridgeway Plaza
P.O. Box 3837
Stamford, CT 06905
203-356-1745

Art Business News is a controlled circulation tabloid format publication aimed at "art dealers, framers and related businesses". It is a good source for information about the fine art poster world. The *Buyer's Guide*, which appears every other August, contains comprehensive industry listings.

Decor
408 Olive St.
St. Louis, MO 63102
314-421-5445

Decor is a well produced glossy magazine aimed at the same business market as *ABN* with perhaps a bit more emphasis on the upper end of the poster industry and on interior decoration. The annual *Sources Directory*, which appears mid-summer, contains comprehensive industry listings.

Greetings Magazine
309 Fifth Avenue
New York, NY 10016
212-679-6677

Greetings is a trade publication which is the self-proclaimed "authority for cards, stationery, gifts, wraps, party goods, novelties and allied products."

New Age Marketing Opportunities Newsletter
P.O. Box 2578
Sedona, AZ 86336
602-282-9574

New Age Marketing Opportunties Newsletter is published six times annually; its "intent is to focus on issues dealing with good marketing buys, resources and pertinent marketing programs for businesses dealing in the New Age marketplace."

Printing News
245 West 17th St.
New York, NY 10011
212-463-6727

Printing News, a trade publication which is "the authoritative weekly newspaper of the printing industry" and "first with the news in the world of graphic communications", is a goldmine of information about trade printers and related suppliers.

Publishing Poynters
Para Publishing
P.O. Box 4232-881
Santa Barbara, CA 93140-4232
805-968-7277 800-PARAPUB

Publishing Poynters is an informative newsletter containing "book marketing news & ideas from Dan Poynter". Actually, much of the content is applicable to the paper products arena. Para Publishing also markets a number of excellent works on book publishing and sponsors workshops given by Mr. Poynter on the topic.

Publishers Weekly
249 W. 17th St.
New York, NY 10011
212-463-6758

Publishers Weekly is the trade publication of the book publishing industry. Of particular interest to paper product publishers is the calendar issue which appears in March.

Step-By-Step graphics
Dynamic Graphics
6000 North Forest Park Drive
Peoria, IL 61656
309-688-8800

Step-By-Step graphics is a bi-monthly glossy how-to magazine aimed at graphic designers, art directors and production managers. Many of the features will be quite informative to the novice in these areas; for example, "The Color OK Challenge", by Jerry Demoney, in the January/February 1987 issue, pp 68-73, gives a good account of what the on press color approval process is like.

3. Professional Associations, Self-Help Groups and Workshops

American Booksellers Association
137 West 25th Street
New York, NY 10001
212-463-8450 800-637-0037

Bookstores are one of the primary outlets for paper products, particularly cards and calendars. The ABA sponsors the leading trade show in the book industry in early June. There is a special section devoted to paper products.

American Society of Magazine Photographers
419 Park Avenue South
New York, NY 10016
212-889-9144

A.R.T.S. Anonymous
P.O. Box 175 Ansonia Station
New York, NY 10023
212-969-0144

This self-help program for "artists recovering through the Twelve Steps" [adopted from the twelve steps of Alcoholics Anonymous] has no dues or fees for membership. "The only requirement for A.R.T.S. membership is a desire to identify and express our creativity."

Artists Career Planning Service
151 First Avenue No. 14
New York, NY 10003
212-460-8163

The Director of this private consulting organization, Peggie Lowenberg, offers workshops, classes and individual help with career and life planning for commercial and fine artists by appointment only.

Arts Information Center
280 Broadway
New York, NY 10007
212-227-0282

Arts Information Center is a non-profit agency which is a clearing house for contemporary fine arts related information; a portfolio review and art gallery referral service are available to artists at a nominal cost.

Debtors Anonymous
General Service Board
P.O. Box 20322
New York, NY 10025-9992

Debtors Anonymous is a self-help program using the twelve steps of Alcoholics Anonymous for those with a problem of compulsive debting. Within the structure of the groups, other financial issues are discussed. Of particular interest are the groups for Business Owners.

Graphic Artists Guild
11 West 20th St.
New York, NY 10011
212-463-7730

This guild represents the interests of illustrators, graphic artists, computer artists and textile designers. They publish pricing and ethical guidelines.

Greeting Card Creative Network
1350 New York Avenue, NW
Washington, DC 20005
202-393-1780

GCCN is "a professional organization formed . . . to respond to the needs of individual artists, writers and photographers working within the greeting card industry."

Self-Publishing for Artists Workshop
c/o Wilderness Studio
299 Pavonia Ave.
Jersey City, NJ 07302
201-659-4554

This workshop, given by Harold Davis and Marcia Keegan provides "all the specifics you need to successfully conceive, create, produce and market your own calendars, cards, books and fine art posters."

4. Printers

Please note: I or those I trust have used the following printers with generally positive results. However, this does not constitute an endorsement of any particular printing company. Nor is there any reason to expect that you will be able to establish a good working relationship with these printers, or that your specific projects will turn out well. To find a printer you might want to contact the industry trade association which represents printers, Printing Industries of America, 1730 N. Lynn St., Arlington, VA 22209, 703-841-8100. While P.I.A. will not supply a membership list, they will refer you to the geographically appropriate unit of their thirty-two local trade associations of printers that can provide further information. Another excellent source of information on printers is the *Directory of Book, Catalog, and Magazine Printers*, 4th Edition, John Kremer, Ad-Lib Publications, Fairfield, IA, 1988, 800-624-5893.

Acme Printing Company
30 Industrial Way
Wilmington, MA 01887
508-658-0800

Bengal Graphics
175 Varick Street
New York, NY 10014
212-924-1762

Concord Litho Co., Inc.
92 Old Turnpike Road
Concord, NH 03301
603-225-3328

Eastern Press, Inc.
P.O. Box 1650
654 Orchard St.
New Haven, CT 06507
203-777-2353

Gardner Lithograph Company
8332 Commonwealth Ave.
Buena Park, CA 90621
213-489-3727

Meriden-Stienhour Press
P.O. Box 159
Lunenberg, VT 05906
802-328-2507

Morgan Press Incorporated
145 Palisade St.
Dobbs Ferry, NY 10522
914-693-0023

Olsen Press Inc.
95 Dermody St.
Cranford, NJ 07016
201-272-4411

Regal Art Press
Industrial Park Road
Troy, NY 12180
518-274-4500

The following companies specialize in producing promotional pieces, brochures and postcards in set sizes and formats. If you have a single item to print, they will strip it together in a standard format with other work to create a flat.

McGrew Color Graphics
1615 Grand Ave.
Kansas City, MO 64141
816-221-6560

MWM Dexter
3046 S Deleware #A
Springfield, MO 65802
417-887-6299; 800-641-4123

Serbin Communications Inc.
614 Santa Barbara St.
Santa Barbara, CA 93101
805-963-0439

Triangle/Expercolor, Inc.
3737 West Chase Avenue
Skokie, IL 60076
312-465-3400

5. Miscellaneous

Artexpo is held in New York at the Jacob Javits Convention Center at the end of March. For further information contact Artexpo, 747 Third Ave., New York, NY 10017, 212-418-4288.

Courier Systems, Inc., 30 Pulaski Street, Bayonne, NJ 07002, 201-432-0550, is a full service fulfillment warehouse.

Light Impressions, 439 Monroe Avenue, Rochester, NY 14607-3717, 1-800-828-6216 (outside NY), 1-800-828-9629 (NY), produces an excellent catalogue of archival supplies and presentation materials.

Moore Business Products, P.O. Box 5000, Vernon Hills, IL 60061, 1-800-323-6230, is a leading mail order supplier of computer forms such as invoices and checks.

National Stationery Show is held in New York at the Jacob Javits Convention Center in May. For further information contact George Little Management, 2 Park Avenue, New York, NY 10016, 212-686-6070.

NEBS, 500 Main Street, Groton, MA 01471, 800-225-9550, produces a catalogue with a general line of inexpensive business stationery and forms.

APPENDIX II

Selected List of Card Companies

American Greetings Corp.
10500 American Rd.
Cleveland, OH 44144
800-242-2737

American Postcard Co.
285 Lafayette St.
New York, NY 10012
212-966-3673

Avanti
800 Penobscot Bldg.
Detroit, MI 48226
800-2-Avanti

Blue Mountain Arts
P.O. Box 4549
Boulder, CO 80306
800-525-0642

Bo-Tree Cards
1137 San Antonio Rd.
Palo Alto, CA 94303
415-967-1817

Fotofolio
536 Broadway, 2nd floor
New York, NY 10012
212-226-0923

Gibson Greeting Cards
2100 Section Rd.
Cincinnati, OH 45237
513-841-6600

Hallmark Cards, Inc.
2501 McGee
Kansas City, MO 64108
816-274-5111

Impact
4961 Windplay Dr.
El Dorado Hills, CA 95630
916-933-4865

Palm Press
1442A Walnut Street #120
Berkeley, CA 94709
415-486-0502

Pomegranate
Box 980
Corte Madera, CA 94925
415-924-8141

Portal Publications
P.O. Box 659
Corte Madera, CA 94925
415-924-5652

Recycled Paper Prod.Inc.
3636 North Broadway
Chicago, IL 60613-6410
312-348-6410

APPENDIX III

Selected Poster Publishers And Publisher/Distributors

Art Beats
251 South Floral St.
Salt Lake City, UT 84111
801-596-2910

Art Leaders, Ltd.
124 East Colorado Blvd.
Pasadena, CA 91105
818-793-7514

Bruce McGaw Graphics, Inc.
230 Fifth Ave.
New York, NY 10001
212-679-7823

Bruce Teleky Inc.
520 Broadway
New York, NY 10012
212-226-0610

Editions Limited Wholesale
625 Second Street
San Francisco, CA 94107
415-543-9811

Front Line Graphics
7696 Formula Pl.
San Diego, CA 92121
619-549-0077

Graphique de France
46 Waltham St.
Boston, MA 02118
617-482-5066

Image Conscious
45 Sheridan
San Francisco, CA 94103
415-626-1555

Image Masters, Inc.
7963 Van Nuys Blvd.
Van Nuys, CA 91402
818-785-8484

Impress Graphics
30 Commerce Road
Stamford, CT 06904
203-348-9494

Mirage Editions Inc.
1659 11th Street
Santa Monica, CA 90404
213-450-1129

Modernart Editions Inc.
80 5th Ave.
New York, NY 10011
212-675-8505

Museum Editions West
2040 Broadway
Santa Monica, CA 90404
213-829-4428

New York Graphic Society
P.O. Box 1469
Greenwich, CT 06836
203-661-2400

Springdale Graphics
911 Hope St.
Springdale, CT 06907
203-356-9510

Waterline Publications
60 K Street
Boston, MA 02127
617-268-8792

The *Directory of Art Publishers, Book Publishers & Record Companies* contains additional listings of publishers and is available by mail from **The Consultant Press,** 163 Amsterdam Avenue #201, New York, N.Y. 10023—$24.95 plus $2.50 for postage and handling.

GLOSSARY

Accounts Payable—Money owed by your company to other businesses, based on the invoices you have received and excluding long-term debt.

Accounts Receivable—Money that is owed to your company, based on valid invoices you have sent and excluding long-term debt.

Aging of Accounts Receivable—A table of accounts receivable, arranged by the amount of time (number of days) from the invoice date.

Blue Print—A photo-print made from the stripped up elements of the offset printing job and used to check correct positioning of the elements.

C.O.D. order—A C.O.D. order is one which must be paid for on a "cash on delivery" basis. When C.O.D. orders are sent via United Parcel Service or other major carriers, a special form needs to be filled out. On this form the shipper can indicate that payment with a company check meets the cash requirement, or else require payment with cash or a certified check.

Commercial Work—Work which an artist or photographer does for money, often as opposed to "personal work", and usually for an advertising agency.

Copyright—A copyright provides the owner, usually the creator in the absence of a work-for-hire agreement, with a number of exclusive rights in the copyrighted work. These rights can be summarized as the right to prevent others from exploiting the work for commercial purposes or for using it in a way which prevents the creator from realizing expected profits. Copyrights maybe registered with the U.S. Copyright Office in which case certain additional presumptions benefit the registrant. Even without registration, however, the creator holds a "common-law" copyright in the work which should be protected by an adequate notice, for example: © Harold Davis 1990.

Delivery Memo—The legal document which accompanies a submission of artwork or photography.

Distributor—A wholesale company whose business is the purchase of goods from various sources and their resale to the trade.

Display face—Large size type face used primarily to get attention and not used as a text face in books.

Factor—A commercial factor lends money to a business using the company accounts receivable as security.

Fine Art Graphic Poster—An offset piece combining image and graphics designed to be sold as art.

Flat—A composite of different images stripped together prior to plate making and designed to be printed on one sheet.

Fulfillment—The warehousing, packing and shipping of finished merchandise.

Hard Copy—A print-out of a computer file.

Invoice—An itemized bill.

Keystone Markup System—A merchandise pricing system under which each entity the product passes through doubles the price.

License—The right to use imagery in a specified way.

Limited Edition Print—A fine art print where the number produced has been strictly limited. Each print should be signed and numbered. Generally, these prints are produced at an atelier using stone lithograph, etching or serigraph techniques. Occasionally, however, photographic prints and those produced via offset are marketed as limited editions.

Linotype service bureau—A company with a linotype machine that converts computer text files and type sets them.

Mechanical—A camera-ready paste-up of artwork. It includes type, photos and artwork or indications for the positioning and cropping of the photos and artwork, line art, etc., in one comprehensible whole.

Net 30 Days—Payment terms on an invoice which means that payment is due in thirty days from the date of the invoice.

Offset—This is the common term for offset-lithography. It is the most widely used kind of quantity reproduction process in printing. Image areas are photoprinted onto a thin metal plate that has been chemically sensitized to accept ink and repel water in the image areas. Non-image areas accept water and repel ink. In offset-lithography, the plate first contacts rollers of water or dampening solution, then the inked rollers. The inked image is then transferred or offset from the plate onto a rubber blanket cylinder, then onto paper.

Packing Slip—Also known as a "Shipping Document" or "Bill of Lading", which accompanies a shipment of merchandise. It itemizes the contents of the shipment and references the customer purchase order and shipper's invoice.

Paper goods—Consumer products, other than books, which are created by printing on paper, for example, calendars, cards and posters.

Plate—A photo-chemically sensitized material, in offset generally made of a thin sheet of metal, which is designed to receive, carry and transfer an inked image.

"PMS" Color—PMS, or Pantone Match System, is a proprietary system designed for specifying non-process colors.

Press Okay—The approval by the client of the printed sheet as it comes off the press.

Process Colors—The primary process colors are Yellow, Magenta and Cyan. First an image must be separated to isolate each of the process colors. Then the three primary process colors are printed in transparent overlays, together with Black, to create the illusion of full color.

Proof—There are many systems of proofs in offset. All are used to check the accuracy of composition, registration and color.

Publisher—A publisher contracts for the right to reproduce work and arranges to have it reproduced, distributed and fulfilled.

Reflected Art—Reflected art, as opposed to transparent art, is opaque and must be photographed by light reflected from its surface. Examples include photographic prints, paintings, ink on paper, etc.

Release—Written permission to publish, utilize, or offer for sale a likeness of a person or of private property.

Retail—A business that sells to the general public. Generally, retailers purchase their inventory from wholesale businesses for 50% of the retail price.

Royalty—Generally, a publisher compensates the creator of a work with a royalty based on a percentage of the retail or wholesale price. Most contracts also provide for a non-refundable advance against royalties.

Sales Commission—A sales commission based on a percentage of actual sales is paid to manufacturer's sales representatives in lieu of salary.

Self-Publish—To be the publisher of one's own work.

Separation—The process by which the colors in full-color originals are separated into the primary printing colors.

Sole Proprietorship—A business that is owned and run by one person; a one person operation.

Statement—A form sent to accounts which lists outstanding invoices and any payments or credits.

Stock agency—An organization that maintains a library of existing works, markets them, and licenses their use for a percentage of the fee collected.

Stock usage—The usage of an existing image.

Template—A standard design format designed to be re-used with new information, for example, on the back of cards.

Trade Credit—The granting of credit by one business to another.

Trade publication—A magazine, newspaper or journal aimed at businesses in a specialized trade, often a controlled circulation publication not sold to the public.

Trade show—A sales exposition aimed at a particular industry. Admission is often limited to those working in the industry.

Transparent art—An image viewed by transmitted, rather than reflected, light; usually a color positive, such as a 35mm slide.

Typositor—A machine that sets type; a typositor shop is a company that uses this machine to set type, particularly display faces.

Unit Cost—What it costs to produce a product; for example, if it costs $10,000 to design and produce 5,000 posters, the unit cost is $2.

Wholesale—Generally, 50% of retail. Wholesale prices are offered to the trade by distributors to retailers.

INDEX